KARL RAHNER

I REMEMBER

KARL RAHNER

I REMEMBER

*An Autobiographical Interview
with Meinold Krauss*

SCM PRESS LTD

Translated by Harvey D. Egan, S.J. from the German
Erinnerungen im Gespräch mit Meinold Krauss
published by Verlag Herder Freiburg im Breisgau
1984

© Verlag Herder Freiburg im Breisgau 1984

English translation © The Crossroad Publishing
Company, New York

Photographs on pages ii and 17 © Adolf Waschel,
Vienna

British Library Cataloguing in Publication Data

Rahner, Karl
  I remember.
  1. Rahner, Karl 2. Catholic Church—Doctrines
  I. Title II. Krauss, Meinhold III. Erinnerugen
  im Gespräch mit Meinhold Krauss. *English*
  230′.2′0924   BX4705.R287

  ISBN 0–334–02083–2

334 02083 2

First British edition published 1985
by SCM Press Ltd
26–30 Tottenham Road, London N1

Typeset in the United States of America
and printed in Great Britain by
The Camelot Press Ltd
Southampton

CONTENTS

TRANSLATOR'S FOREWORD

"Strengthened by the Church's sacrament and accompanied by the prayers of his Jesuit brothers, shortly after completing his eightieth year, Father Karl Rahner has gone home to God. . . . He had loved the Church and his religious order and spent himself in their service." So reads part of the official Jesuit announcement of the death of Father Karl Rahner, S.J., on March 30, 1984. And with his death, the Church has lost one of her most loyal sons. Although well known for his often controversial reinterpretations of the Christian tradition and for his criticisms of much in the Church's practical life, Rahner always spoke from deep within the Church as one who had never lost sight of the total Christian vision.

Born the middle of seven children of a teachers' college professor and a "courageous" mother on March 5, 1904, in Freiburg, West Germany, Father Rahner had been a Jesuit for sixty-two years, a priest for fifty-two, and led a "theological life" for almost forty-five. He had taught theology at Innsbruck, Munich, and Münster, and had lectured all over the world. Four thousand written works, paperback sales in excess of one million copies, backbreaking editorial work on theological encyclope-

The following is a revision of my "A Friend Remembers Karl Rahner's 'Theological Life'," *Homiletic and Pastoral Review*, January 1985, pp. 60–64.

1

dias and reference works, as well as several volumes of television, radio, and newspaper interviews, make up his bibliography.

Not only had Rahner written on almost every significant theological topic, but he had also entered into dialogue with Protestant, Jewish, Muslim, Buddhist, Marxist, atheistic, and scientific thinkers the world over. His unanswered questions have provided fresh points of departure for a host of lesser thinkers. Add to this his significant impact upon the Second Vatican Council, his fourteen honorary doctoral degrees, and the large number of doctoral students he directed, and one can see how aptly he has been called "the quiet mover of the Roman Catholic Church" and "the Father of the Catholic Church in the twentieth century." Yet Rahner referred to himself as someone who was "not particularly industrious," who "went to bed early," and was a "poor sinner." "All I want to be, even in this work [of theology], is a human being, a Christian, and, as well as I can, a priest of the Church."

Although Thomas Aquinas, Heidegger, Kant, Hegel, and Maréchal undoubtedly influenced his thinking, Rahner contended that the great Christian mystics and saints, as well as the Jesuit spirituality he prayed and lived, had a much greater significance for his theological work. For him the saints were theological sources. He saw clearly that the faith of the theologian as well as the living faith of the contemporary Church were both crucial to the theological enterprise. From him I learned that theology can be distinguished, but never separated from living faith, hope, and love. Theology must flow out of and then lead back into the prayer of silent surrender to the Mystery of God's love for us in the crucified and risen Christ— *and* must do so without dissolving theology's necessarily critical function. The theologian must have compassion for the human and worship God with his whole person, knowing when to "kneel his mind" before the incomprehensible God, whose love became manifestly irreversible in Christ's life, death, and resurrection.

Central to Rahner's thinking is the notion that what is at the core of every person's deepest experience, what haunts every human heart, is a God whose mystery, light, and love have embraced the total person. God works in every person's life as the One to whom we say our inmost yes or no. We may deny this, ignore it, or repress it, but deep down we know that God is in love with us and we are all at least secretly in love with one another. Therefore, one of theology's most important functions is "mystagogical." It must lead persons into their own deepest mystery by awakening, deepening, and explicating what every person already lives. It must challenge persons to grasp the real meaning of their freedom as total response to or rejection of the demands of God's love for nothing less than complete human authenticity. And because God has conquered the human heart through the pierced and risen heart of Jesus Christ, Rahner can state the *hope* that all will be saved.

In fact, Rahner contended that the most important achievement of the Second Vatican Council was its *optimistic* attitude toward salvation, its implicit recognition of "anonymous Christianity." This means that even the agnostic or atheist "who courageously accepts life . . . has already accepted God. For anyone who really accepts *himself* accepts . . . the One who has decided to fill this infinite emptiness (which is the mystery of the human person) with his own infinite fullness (which is the mystery of God)."

That he has been designated *Doctor Mysticus*, the Doctor of twentieth-century Mystical Theology, is indeed fitting. Much of Rahner's theology can be called "mystical" because it takes seriously the *experience*, albeit often hidden or repressed, of God's self-communication. The experience of God forms the undertow, or the basal spiritual metabolism, of daily life. Because this is so, no one can escape being a theologian. So, Rahner chided academicians for ducking the key question of human existence: "Is life absurd?" Rahner addresses the question and answers it in the negative, for "the human person is a being who does not live absurdly because he loves, . . . hopes, and because God, the holy mystery, is infinitely receptive and accepting of him." In view of this, much of Rahner's theology may be called "mystical" because it attempts to compress, to simplify, and to concentrate all Christian beliefs and practices by indicating how they evoke the experience of God's loving self-communication to us in the crucified and risen Christ. Even the agnostic or atheist who loves in courageous fidelity to the demands of everyday life lives the "mysticism of daily life."

For Rahner, moreover, "all life is a subject of theological reflection." Impelled by his "Ignatian mysticism of joy in the world" and of "finding God in all things," Rahner's theology also contains a movement of "unfolding" the mystery of God's suffering and victorious love for us in Christ into every dimension of human life. Has any other contemporary theologian written a "theology of everyday things"—a theology of work, of getting about, sitting down, seeing, laughing, eating, sleeping, and the like? Nothing here below is profane for those who know how to see. And if his theology of mystical compression often involves anfractuous dialectics dealing with questions such as the Trinity, the Incarnation, the problem of evil, and so on, his theology of unfolding can be as lovely as advising an unwed mother in her darkest hour to look into the face of her newborn son for light.

Perhaps the secret of Rahner's appeal is his synthesis of two elements: critical respect for Christian tradition and unusual sensitivity to the questions and problems of contemporary life. He never overlooked how difficult Christian faith is for a twentieth-century person. But he could and did say to his contemporaries not only, "I am also someone who has been tempted by atheism," but also, "There is nothing more self-evident to me than God's existence." Therefore, Rahner would accept nothing less from theology than speaking about God, not just so-called God-talk, while breathing the air of unbelief.

Moreover, Rahner never doubted the ability of Christianity's profound tradition to say what was necessary for authentic contemporary living. Because of his ability to discover *the tradition* in the traditions, Rahner was able to revitalize even some of the oldest "fossils" of Christian creeds, dogmas, and beliefs into living realities. He sought "the dearest freshness deep down things." How do the old "keys" of faith fit the various "locks" to release contemporary human authenticity? Rahner demanded that theology be a science of conversion, faith, and prayer that deepens the way people live their faith, hope, and love.

In so many ways, therefore, Rahner's theology is preeminently *pastoral*. Perhaps it was his pastoral work in war-ravaged Europe during and after the Second World War that gave him his spontaneous inclination toward the pastoral care of individuals and the concerns of a Church in "diaspora." In fact, many of his writings are essays written for particular occasions or in response to questions as they arose, not the overly systematic and encyclopedic approach considered typical of German theologians his age. One of the most absurd statements I ever read about Rahner's theology was that there was nothing priestly, kerygmatic, or pastoral about it. It should be said of him that his theology is supremely pastoral and its major focus: "Salus animarum suprema lex" (The salvation of souls is the supreme law).

Prodded by the insights of Johann Baptist Metz, one of his former students, Rahner, moving in the direction of liberation and political theology, developed his well-known thesis that love of neighbor *is* love of God. If we really believe in the Gospel, how will we treat others and transform society? What is the Church, and what should it be doing in this regard? For Rahner, the social-political ramifications of the Gospel need particular emphasis today.

During an interview a few days before his eightieth birthday, a journalist asked Rahner his views on old age. Rahner replied that a person should never stop thinking, and that if God gives one strength to write in old age, one should receive it as a gift. Rahner saw old age as a chance to sum up one's entire life, to get oneself together before the final Mystery. And when the journalist persisted in questioning him about the fear of death, Rahner replied: "I have the right as a man, a Christian, and a theologian to be afraid of this dark event. . . . I hope to have the strength to surrender lovingly into the great Mystery of God's love which embraces it."

I first met Father Rahner in 1969 when he graciously accepted the invitation to concelebrate my first Mass with me and to spend the day with my family and friends. During my four years of doctoral studies under his direction, I found him to be at once utterly brilliant, shockingly creative, traditional, original, provocative, balanced, and healing. A passion for hard work, detail, precision, and an impatience with mental laziness, "whoring after relevance," and bureaucratic incompetence stamped his personality. However, most impressive of all were his childlike curiosity and the simplicity, holiness, and priestliness of his Jesuit and theological life.

Father Rahner had an uncanny ability when it came to finding money, food, clothing, and shelter for the needy and downtrodden who sought him out. He possessed the knack, too, of shanghaiing others into assisting him with his practical works of charity. One of the things I remember most vividly is how we two went grocery shopping in a large supermarket and drove two hours to take the food to a widow and to find her a place to live. One of Rahner's last public acts after the celebration of his eightieth birthday was to appeal for funds to purchase a motorcycle for a missionary in Africa.

The countless ways in which he brought meaning, comfort, light, relief, and healing to so many persons prompted one distinguished German author to call Rahner a "most effective psychotherapist." For example, I know how priestly and generous with his time Rahner was to a young Jesuit friend who was leaving the priesthood. Students who understood very little of his lectures told me that they attended because they "felt better" about themselves in his presence. "This is a professor to whom I can confess," one said. Not many years before his death, Rahner often spent several hours of his intensely busy day helping a young German psychiatrist to recover some of the memory he had lost in a serious auto accident.

Shortly before Father Rahner died in March of 1984, I had just finished reading his *Karl Rahner im Gespräch*, two-volumes of his television, radio, and newspaper interviews from 1964 to 1982. These interviews had a tremendous effect on me because of how much they revealed about Rahner the man and how much they intensified an ever-present awareness of how indebted to him I am for my theological and spiritual life.

When I heard the news of his death, I must admit candidly that I did not grieve for very long. Unlike the long, protracted, humiliating death of Father Bernard Lonergan, another great theologian and close friend, Father Rahner was able to work right up to the end. Also, his death was relatively quick and painless. So I rejoice in the Lord for him that he went into eternal life with a blaze of glory.

However, an ever-increasing desire to return to Germany and Austria began to haunt me. Even my dreams became filled with Rahner episodes. It soon became apparent that a Rahner-pilgrimage was necessary for my own peace of mind. So in the summer of 1984 I went to Germany and Austria with the great desire to talk with people who were with Rahner when he was dying, to visit some of his old haunts and his family in Freiburg, to reestablish contact with various Rahner scholars, to use his archives at Innsbruck, and to pray at his crypt in the Jesuit church in Innsbruck. All those with whom I spoke attested repeatedly to one thing about Rahner: the awesome way in which his spirit shone forth in faith, courage, and intelligence right up to the very evening he died.

Precisely because Rahner said that he would write neither his autobiography nor memoirs, the Reverend Meinold Krauss, in collaboration with Germany's Channel 2 (ZDF), ought to be commended for prodding Rahner into giving this lengthy, sustained reflection on his life. This interview contains material found nowhere else, is highly autobiographical, and is Rahner at his most personal and intimate—a rare treat, especially for those who knew him well.

Since 1962 I have been reading Rahner's works. With the exception of a few interviews he gave in East-bloc countries shortly before his death, I have read everything he has written. I have likewise been giving courses and seminars on his thought since 1973. But despite my professional and personal involvement with Rahner for over twenty years, and despite my feelings at the time of his death and shortly thereafter, the power with which this interview possessed my spirit astonished me. Although I dislike translation work, I admit candidly that I felt "called" to translate this extremely important interview which was completed only a short time before he died.

This interview vividly captures the Rahner I came to know and love for almost a quarter century. It communicates the spirit of Rahner the man, the priest, the Jesuit, the theologian, and the Christian known and admired by so many people. Some of my students have said that Rahner makes even the most obscure Christian dogma meaningful, that he brings to intelligible articulation the living catechism of the heart of so many contemporary people—and not only of Christians. And I fully agree, for I have long contended that theology cannot be separated from the theologian, that theology *is* ultimately the person who theologizes. Hence, I always ask myself whenever I read theology: "What kind of person wrote this?" Therefore, I am certain that what compelled me to translate this interview was nothing less than the spirit of Rahner which it evokes and communicates so effectively.

For this reason, I cannot recommend this book highly enough to anyone with any interest in Karl Rahner. It is the easiest, most readable way into his mind and heart. It is also the book that reveals the most about Rahner the man, the priest, the Jesuit, the theologian, and the Christian. It can serve both as an introduction to Rahner's thought and as the last will and testament of the Father of Roman Catholic theology in the twentieth century. It is a "must" for anyone interested in Rahner.

The Germans have a tradition of presenting a person celebrating some special occasion with a *Festschrift*, an honorary publication written by others. Rahner, at age twenty-four, and his brother Hugo had written one for their father on the occasion of his sixtieth birthday. Therefore, I see my translation as a labor of love, as my *Festschrift* to my *Doktorvater*, to a man I grew to love as more than a theologian. And if Rahner had the audacity and humility to write a letter in Saint Ignatius's name to contemporary Jesuits, I felt a similar need to put myself in Rahner's place and ask: "How would Rahner say this to an American audience?" Rahner's love of understatement, indirection, double negatives, conditional sentences, multiple adverbs, and the like, did not make this an easy task.

For this reason I want to thank Daniel Shine, S.J., Martin Rauch, S.J., Michael Skelley, S.J., and Colleen Webster for reading the entire manuscript and for their valuable suggestions.

Finally, I have often emphasized that Rahner's theology begins and ends in prayer. That Rahner began his writing career, for all practical purposes, with a book on prayer, *Encounters with Silence*, and ended it with *Prayers for a Lifetime* emphasizes this point.* In fact, explicit prayers and penetrating reflection on prayer punctuated his entire theological life. Even many essays in his meaty *Theological Investigations* often end by shading into prayer. Thus, Rahner stands in a long line of great Christian theologians who were likewise great teachers

---

*Encounters with Silence, translated by James M. Demske, S.J. (Westminster, Md.: The Newman Press, 1960); *Prayers for a Lifetime*, edited by Albert Raffelt, with an introduction by Karl Lehmann (New York: Crossroad, 1984).

of prayer. In view of everything above, and especially this final point, I wish to end this foreword by calling Rahner *Doctor Orationis*, the Doctor of Prayer for the twentieth century. So, is it any wonder that often, since his death, I have found myself praying not only for Rahner but *to* Rahner?

Father of my theological life and of my heart, may you be plunged more deeply into the Mystery of God, be enlightened by his crucified and risen Son, and burn with the love of the Holy Spirit. Help us to live in daily humdrum love with courage, to look upon the Crucified, and to be ready to die into the holy Incomprehensibility of God when it is our time. Meet with us daily in the Eucharist. Amen.

Harvey D. Egan, S.J.

INTERVIEWER'S PREFACE

ROMAN STORIES

To question Karl Rahner about his life and work in front of a television camera seemed to me to be something urgently needed in the present as well as for posterity. I first attempted this early in 1979. On the occasion of his seventy-fifth birthday, I was to produce a profile on Rahner for television. After hesitating for a long time ("Who'll be interested in what I'll say there?") Rahner agreed and we were to film him in Munich and Rome. We flew to Rome intending to record a meeting between Professor Rahner and Pope John Paul II. However, our efforts in this matter were in vain. To be sure, Rahner did have a private audience with the pope, without requesting it, but filming or the taking of pictures was not allowed.

Propriety forbade my asking Professor Rahner how the conversation went. Rahner later spoke about it a bit under the rubric, "How one can speak with the pope." "Since I knew the pope from a luncheon with him in Cracow, his first question when he shook my hand at the audience was: 'How are you?' I was unprepared and flustered and said: 'Oh, I'm emeritus now, living in Munich, and waiting for death.' This answer apparently didn't faze the pope. He said only: 'One says in Poland: "Some must; others can."' I don't exactly

12

know what he meant by that. Presumably, I would soon be one of those who 'must.' Actually one shouldn't speak with popes about one's own death. They have other concerns."

After the papal audience we were invited to lunch with the Jesuit General, Pedro Arrupe. During the table talk the conversation turned to an illustrated book on Saint Ignatius, in which Rahner has the saint speak to today's Jesuits.* Arrupe asked with interest about the book's success. "It's selling very well and has been translated into several languages," Rahner replied. "Well," said Arrupe, "It has some lovely pictures."

Change of scene: In the Vatican gardens we quickly and satisfactorily wrapped up a ten-question interview. There was to be no filming that afternoon, so Rahner took the opportunity to show me a few of the Eternal City's art treasures that I had never seen before. The excursion ended in the Piazza Navona where Rahner invited me for ice cream and said that during the Council he had often gotten "a good ice cream" there with Cardinal Volk.

On the way back to the hotel, Rahner told me about his first meeting with Cardinal Ottaviani in Rome and about a later meeting in Innsbruck: "I traveled with the Cardinal in his Mercedes from Innsbruck to Munich for a eucharistic congress. On the trip, Ottaviani said the rosary and also recited the Litany of Loreto out loud in Latin and by heart. I joined in. To be sure, he had imposed a special Roman censor on me for any new writings, but we were able to pray very well together. He was a great man, too." An unforgettable day for me, rich in conversation and adventures, ended in Rome on that 14th of March 1979.

***Ignatius of Loyola*, by Karl Rahner, S.J., with an Historical Introduction by Paul Imhof and color photographs by Helmut Loose (New York: Collins, 1979).

WITNESS OF THE CENTURY

The day I arrived in Innsbruck with the ZDF television team for the series "Witnesses of the Century" was also unforgettable. Two things were especially important: to find a suitable room for the filming and to hit upon some device that could serve as a "discussion starter" for the interview. According to ZDF instructions, the filming should "usually be done in the locale, in the very ambience, of the one being interviewed." However, we could not follow this recommendation because Rahner's office, filled with book shelves, offered no space for the TV camera and other equipment. Finally, after a bit of looking around, we decided to set up in the room of the rector of the university. Its venerable baroque furniture certainly had nothing in common with Rahner's daily life. Still, we put up with this "falsification" for the sake of a larger room for the TV equipment.

After this "search for motif," Professor Rahner led me to his office and asked with Alemannian slyness if one could compare a theologian to an atomic physicist. When I couldn't think of an answer, Rahner showed me a cartoon that had been sent to him anonymously. How the comparison came about can be seen on page 18.

It was suddenly clear to me that this caricature could indeed be the "discussion starter" for our talk. And so we began with it. At first Rahner acted rather reserved, almost unfriendly. His contracted facial expression seemed the mirror image of his mental concentration. However, when a smile illuminated this serious face, his goodness, affection, and lovableness became strikingly apparent. Mario von Galli's characterization of Karl Rahner's "grumpy charm" hit the mark.

It was not easy to question Professor Rahner about himself

and others in front of the camera, especially since he loved understatement. Self-praise was totally foreign to him, and one sensed that this first-rate scholar had remained a simple man and an unpretentious Christian. And something else was also striking: As only few can, Rahner could be just as astonished by the engineering of an elevator as by the Trinity. And the most important thing: You could really talk with him about everything, about God and the world.

BUT THE END WOULD BE THE SILENCE...

"God in the world" is the short formula Rahner invoked for his theology at one time. He used it to point out to more than one generation of theologians, and not only of his own Church, a direction in which new discoveries, surprises, and experiences are to be found. In the years ahead, when one comes to write the history of twentieth-century theology, Karl Rahner's name will play a significant and literally decisive role. There will certainly be no unanimity even then as to how to judge his theological initiatives. But no one will dispute his rank, that unique key position that only very few in any discipline ever attain. Certainly Karl Rahner plays this key role in twentieth-century Catholic theology. In February 1984, his authority and authenticity were clearly renewed in a completely filled auditorium at the University of Freiburg when he gave his supposedly last public lecture on the occasion of his forthcoming eightieth birthday. Shortly after that he traveled abroad to give more lectures.

One day after his birthday on March 5, which he celebrated with friends and students, he had to be brought to the hospital, where he died during the night of March 30, 1984. During the burial Mass at the Jesuit church in Innsbruck, words from 1 Corinthians were read: "For our knowledge is imperfect and our prophecy is imperfect. But when the perfect comes, the imperfect will pass away."

While listening to these words, I was instinctively reminded of Karl Rahner's words written almost as a spiritual epilogue a few months earlier: "I have said much and spoken of many things. And still I forgot much and left much unsaid that you or others wished to hear from me. I do not want to list again the themes that I could just as well have said something about as those I actually did address. But the end in both cases would be the silence in which the eternal praise of God takes place."

Meinold Krauss

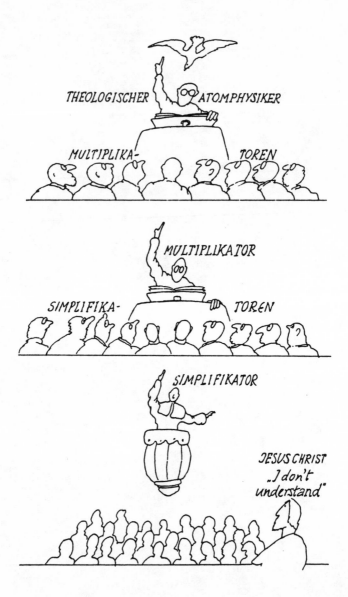

"A THEOLOGICAL
ATOMIC PHYSICIST"

KRAUSS:
Professor Rahner, when you published a book a short time ago, this cartoon was sent to you anonymously. What is it about?

RAHNER:
As you see, at the top of the cartoon is a theological atomic physicist who's supposed to be me. What it means is that I speak about things that no one understands. Beneath me sit the so-called multipliers. They are the ones who are expected to hand on what I say. Beneath them sit the popularizers who spend their time putting what the multipliers say into simple language. Below them, in the pulpit, is an individual popularizer who preaches to the Christian people what needs to be said there. Nearby sits Jesus Christ who listens to what is being translated from what I've concocted, and he says: "I don't understand." That's just the way it is when you're a theology teacher.

DECIDING TO
BECOME A THEOLOGIAN

KRAUSS:

Professor Rahner, if one looks over your life's work up to now, as far as one can do that at all, it is easy to see why some people are inclined to characterize you as "a theological atomic physicist." You yourself once said that you never wanted to be a theologian at all, that you only wanted to be an ordinary man, a Christian, and a priest of your church in everything you say, write, or do.

Anyone who knows you understands how passionate you are about being not only a scholar, not only a theologian, but also and above all else a pastor, and that the goal of your theological work is ultimately to make the good news of Christianity so clear to today's searchers and questioners that even they could say: "A person today can believe and understand that." Professor Rahner, how did you come to be a theologian? What was the beginning of your theological journey?

RAHNER:

Well, I grew up with six other children in a perfectly normal Christian family—Catholic but not bigoted. I attended a regular secondary school, obtained my diploma there, and then entered the Jesuits. And if you do that, then you want to become a priest and want to be a member of a religious community. The mission of the Society of Jesus is ministry and missions, the preaching of the Gospel at home and in actual missionary lands. And so, through developments that occurred to me in the Society, and without going into it in greater detail, I eventually and finally landed in theology.

That was a perfectly normal career available to a German Jesuit in addition to other possibilities. Obviously, in a religious order a superior directs one's career. It was initially intended that I become a professor of the history of philosophy within the teaching activities of the Jesuits. That was my destiny, as we used to say, as decided by my religious superiors through the long years of my studies. Strictly speaking, it was only after I was ordained a priest and had expressly returned to the study of philosophy that I was suddenly "redestined," as we say, to become a theology professor on the theological faculty at the University of Innsbruck. But there was nothing strange about this.

During my six semesters of philosophy within the Society and my four of philosophy at the University of Freiburg, and throughout eight semesters of normal theological education, I always remained interested in theology. That I was consequently redirected from the history of philosophy to dogmatic theology corresponded completely with my own inclinations and wishes, especially since I really wasn't interested in scholarship for the sake of scholarship. My needs and outlook were completely, immediately, and genuinely pastoral—at least, so I believe. Perhaps this outlook was always a bit oriented toward a somewhat educated audience. I don't say this proudly but self-critically. Since I was a Jesuit, I had the vague notion that I might one day become a student chaplain, but that I should just become a university professor of theology was completely beyond my own horizon and intentions.

This "redestination" allowed me, then, to stay in theology. To a certain extent at least I could and would have to do scholarly work in theology too, but I think that ultimately my theological work was really not motivated by scholarship and erudition as such, but by pastoral concerns. This likewise explains why a large part of my published work is filled with immediately religious, spiritual, and pastoral concerns. It also explains why in my theology and in my individual works— aside from my research into the history of dogma, which *is* scholarly—I have always chosen, and in fact had to choose, tasks and themes that somehow dealt with the actual moment, with the questions of our day. And this explains, too, why a large portion of my theological output—if I may say so—sixteen volumes of *Schriften zur Theologie**—is made up of individual essays on the most diverse subjects, prompted, as they certainly were, by the concrete conditions of the time, the Church, and pastoral need.

For example, the fact that I wrote an article many years ago about Christians and their unbelieving relatives, which attracted much interest, shows very clearly that pastoral motivations were behind my work. The same holds true, for example, for my book *Happiness Through Prayer* or, if I remember correctly, the two volumes of lectures on the *Spiritual Exercises* of Saint Ignatius of Loyola, the founder of the Jesuits. Likewise, the essential thrust of my theological work becomes rather

---

*Volumes 1 to 14 of the *Schriften* correspond to volumes 1 to 20 of *Theological Investigations* (with volume 7 each of the German volumes was split into two volumes in English). Since 1961 *Theological Investigations* has been published by Darton, Longman & Todd in England and has appeared under a number of imprints in the United States: first, Helicon Press, then Herder and Herder, The Seabury Press, and finally The Crossroad Publishing Company. All twenty volumes are currently available from Crossroad, and translations of German volumes 15 and 16 are in preparation.

clear, I believe, in *The Practice of Faith*, an anthology of my writings on spiritual themes, edited by Karl Lehmann and Albert Raffelt.*

KRAUSS:
Can one say, therefore, that you became a theologian under rather strange circumstances? That your religious superior destined you to study philosophy in order for you to assume a professorship in philosophy, but all the same, from the beginning your deepest inclination was more theological than philosophical?

RAHNER:
Yes, certainly. If one becomes a Jesuit, then one doesn't want to become a professor of philosophy, but someone who ministers to people, a priest, a member of a religious order. Moreover, when I entered the Jesuit novitiate, I had to be prepared to be sent to the North American Indians or to work pastorally somewhere in Brazil. Many who entered the novitiate with me are now either in India—of course they are now pretty old—or in Brazil. That could have happened to me too. I had to face that from the beginning. The notion that one becomes a Jesuit to become a learned professor is actually quite misleading.

*New York: Crossroad, 1983.

A PERFECTLY NORMAL
CHRISTIAN FAMILY

KRAUSS:

Professor Rahner, how much did your parents consciously or unconsciously shape you? When you think over your past way of life, what do you owe to your parents?

RAHNER:

I grew up, I must say, in a normal, middle-class, Christian family. My father was what is today called an assistant principal; then they were known as "Baden professors." For most of his life he was a professor at the teachers' college in Freiburg. My mother came from an innkeepers' family. My grandparents had a small hotel on the outskirts of Freiburg. And there were seven children in my immediate family, as I've already said.

One could also say, to be more precise, that I grew up in a middle- to lower-middle-class family. The salaries of officials at that time were very modest. For example, in 1904/5, at the time I was born, my father had to spend around one-third of his pay just for the rented apartment that we first had in Emmendingen in the vicinity of Freiburg. But we always had enough to eat. We always had enough clothing. But we had no opportunity for upward mobility. My mother baby-sat to bring in some extra money. My father had to tutor on the side to support seven children who eventually attended university-oriented secondary schools, and all of whom, I believe, got diplomas and went to study at a university.

Two of my brothers are doctors. One brother was a teacher at a business school. My oldest sister married a lawyer from Hamburg. My youngest sister married a mathematician who worked for a long time at the technical high school in Aachen. All this was somehow normal, I'd like to think. It was a lifestyle common to the middle class fifty, sixty, eighty years ago. My grandfather was a teacher in a small village near Freiburg. He also served as the community clerk in order to earn enough to feed his three children and to send two of them to the university. My aunt, my father's sister, was a real farm girl on a Black Forest farm in the same village.

In this kind of family, a child grows up with few problems really. What one is expected to do and not to do is somehow or other perfectly clear. At that time, there was very little about which to be introspective. We really didn't experience serious difficulties. I never saw my parents fight. In the milieu in which I grew up, there was never any talk about divorce among my relatives and acquaintances. All the things that are problems today—a lack of respect for authority, marital problems, problems of sexual morality, and the like— the whole crisis of growing up did not yet exist. Certainly, after the First World War, let's say, much of this was already beginning.

When my brother began to study medicine in 1924, people said to him: "How in the world will you manage to study medicine? You won't be able to earn enough for the water in the soup"! When I was growing up, times were different— necessarily so, I believe—from what they are now. Of course, I did attend a middle-class secondary school. At that time we already had boys and girls in the same class from the fourth level on. Even then this was no problem, at least not in Baden.

We also had pupils from the most varied social classes and backgrounds, naturally Jews as well. This too was absolutely no problem. I remember especially a Jewish boy who got along perfectly with his classmates. His father was an important dealer in leather goods in Hamburg. Obviously, various religious denominations were also represented. Again, this was simply not a problem. We went to our Catholic religious instructions, and there in all our classes we had a very intelligent, educated, reasonable, if somewhat dry, religion teacher who had studied at the Germanicum in Rome and was formed accordingly.

My family was in one way or another clearly Catholic and Christian—practicing Christian at that. Originally my mother may have set the tone more than my father, but that too wasn't a particular problem. In short, if someone grows up in a family like this and decides on a vocation, perhaps without being strongly influenced from elsewhere, then the decision to become a priest, a Jesuit, isn't really a big step.

No one else in my whole family, except my brother Hugo, thought of becoming a priest, which shows that our outlook was not particularly clerical. But as I have said, this too was no big problem. At first I told my parents nothing about my plans to become a Jesuit. The Alemannian Germans of my region are rather reserved in this regard. They don't speak easily about things like that. As it happened, my parents learned of my intention from my religion teacher. He said: "No, Karl isn't suited for that. He's too withdrawn and grumpy. He should become something else." Well, by God, it happened all the same, and has lasted for sixty years. But it does show that this thoroughly Christian family atmosphere was still not of the sort to shape a person in a narrowly clerical way by hook or by crook.

KRAUSS:

It is easy for me to see that you had a very good home life, one that you can look back upon with gratitude. But I find it hard to believe that even then the world, society, was in such good order that there weren't even marriage problems, that the problems of sexuality, of raising children, and of the whole development of society should not have played a role. Rather, couldn't it be that when you were growing up people lived more sheltered lives? That people did not discuss their problems and difficulties openly and honestly? That there were broken marriages in your day as well? That people didn't want to admit it or simply hid it from outsiders because what *ought* not to be simply *could* not be?

RAHNER:

Yes, there can be no doubt that there were problems of the sort you mention in the world even sixty, eighty years ago. One needs only to look at the books of the period. And it's also not as if things like that went quite unnoticed within my own family. I dimly remember when the first rumors of Einstein's theory of relativity appeared in my secondary school years. I also remember how people discussed Spengler's *Decline of the West*, and I recall that as a high schooler I was in an Ibsen play. Of course the things you described existed in my day. But somehow or other the world still seemed more stable. People knew what they had to do and, on the whole, acted accordingly.

Naturally there were human problems. When I was ten years old, the First World War began. And I can still remember it very well. My two elder brothers were soldiers in that war. The oldest was rather seriously wounded and my mother, on her own, fetched him out of some hospital and brought him back to Freiburg. Other relatives fell in battle. Soldiers returned from the war who obviously had had experiences like those described in Remarque's *All Quiet on the Western Front*. But for the most part life was simpler and more stable in those days.

I can still recall our patriotic enthusiasm. We used to mark the western front on a map with a pen, and as a teenager I was one of the boys who in 1918 had to help the Freiburg Soldiers' Council clear away magazines and things like that. I still remember it all rather well, and it taught me a certain lesson: how quickly the glory of this world can pass.

I was born in a monarchy. My father was an official of the grand duke of Baden. We celebrated the Kaiser's birthday. We pinned on blue cornflowers. We put nails in a tree in Freiburg to commemorate the war dead. We were put up at the university because our own high school was a hospital. Consequently, one noticed early on how life can have its dark sides.

KRAUSS:

You spent your schoolboy years in Freiburg, where you also belonged to a youth organization. What significance did your membership in that group have for you at the time?

RAHNER:

Yes, I belonged to an organization called "Fountain of Youth." It was more of a grass-roots than a church-directed affair. But it was still Catholic, religious, extremely active and intense. There too I received many positive influences that affected my future life, especially since that was when I first met Romano Guardini at Castle Rothenfels.

KRAUSS:

What were the young Karl Rahner's dreams as he enthusiastically participated in this youth organization?

RAHNER:

I no longer remember that in detail. One wanted to be a Christian believer experientially and with genuine religious initiative. But what were the ideals then of a sixteen or seventeen-year old boy who intended to become a priest? At that age one's ideals are certainly not narrow or bigoted. However, they were obviously influenced one way or another by the Catholic milieu of the time.

KRAUSS:

Professor Rahner, I want to return to your particularly pleasant and secure childhood and youth. Do you wish that things today could be as they were then? Or would you admit without reservation that we live this way today and must accept the fact that things were, after all, much different years ago?

RAHNER:

Obviously, there is much that once was that cannot be revived and renewed in any way. Of course not. My brothers', sisters', and nephews' families are totally different today. For instance, I get along very well with one of my nephews, the son of my youngest sister. He is a doctor, actually a researcher in human genetics in Heildelberg. That his family is quite different, that they live and will grow up quite differently from the way we did is a foregone conclusion.

But I simply can't give you a recipe for transposing the best from the good old days into today's world. I don't know how. I really do not know how today's children should be raised. I really do not know how married people should live today in contrast to earlier times. Of course now there are problems like how many children one should have and so on that my parents obviously did not have. My mother's brother also had six children. At the time, to have fewer than three or four children was rare. So I cannot offer words of advice. Everyone must live in his or her own time and deal with it. And I believe that the ultimate truths of the faith and of Christianity's basic inspiration can still be absolutely important for us today in coping with life as it now is and must be.

KRAUSS:

In *God in the World*, the *Festschrift* written in your honor and presented to you on your sixtieth birthday, your brother Hugo (about whom we will speak later) wrote that you revered both your parents in a special way and were indebted to them. One way you expressed this was to prepare a private *Festschrift* for your father on the occasion of his sixtieth birthday when you were merely twenty-four. Later on you did something similar for your mother. Professor Rahner, do you still remember the moment when you presented your parents with these extraordinary gifts?

RAHNER:

I cannot possibly remember the exact moment because I was already in the Jesuits at the time and in those days we were not allowed to go home before ordination—hence, ten years after entering. As far as I can recall, my brother simply sent the *Festschrift*, typed and nicely-bound essays from the both of us, to my father through the mail.

I would like to add that in those days people were less emotional, I believe, and less given to expressing their feelings, less eager for intense experiences than is the case today. One grew up in a family of seven children who needed care. They also needed money if they were to study at the university. In those days, to some degree, one had neither the explicit desire nor the time to create the comforts of home. But they were there all the same.

I can't remember any special signs of parental affection toward me. Everything then was more uncluttered emotionally, more sober. If a mother had to get up at 6 A.M. to see to the washing and had to care not only for seven children and a husband but for four or more other people as well, even if she had, for all it's worth, the help of servants, or if a French captain lived with us to learn German in order to make the General Staff, or the son of an English lord who also wished to learn German (why? I no longer know), then one had little time to cultivate feelings. And one had little need of them, either.

Of course we children were closely knit, even though there was as much as a sixteen-year age gap between us. My oldest sister was my youngest brother's godmother. Children romp and fight, right? Naturally we loved each other, if one wants to use this pompous word. But in those days there were few problems; at most the kind that everyone has.

For example, my mother looking back in her later years said that she might have given too little affection and warmth to her children, and things like that. Perhaps that was so, but at the time we did not pay this much attention. My father may have gotten angry when one of us got poor grades. Yet for all practical purposes, my parents did not really concern themselves with their children's progress at school, how they related to teachers, and so on, although my father was himself a teacher. At that time, one went to school, one crammed, got grades, and tried to get by. But for the most part, again, there were no great problems.

KRAUSS:

You were born in Freiburg in Breisgau on March 5, 1904. And your father, Professor Karl Rahner, and your mother, Frau Luise Rahner, née Drescher, came from the Freiburg area, too. That makes you Alemannian German like Karl Barth, Martin Heidegger, Bernard Welte, and Max Müller. People say about the Alemannians that they are pensive, taciturn, and work like horses. Do you agree?

RAHNER:

I have nothing against this characterization. I find it quite honorable and lovely. However, if it doesn't please others as much, that doesn't bother me either. By and large, what you say is correct. The Black Forest German is less lively, less on the *qui vive* than the Swabian—that means less hasty and maybe less intent on keeping up with the Joneses than other Germans. He is at peace with himself one way or the other. Live and let live, he says. To some extent, he is, as you said, a bit pensive. But, of course, you can also find variations within this regional type. I never cared much for wine. My friend Bernard Welte is an extraordinary connoisseur of Baden wine. Certainly there are variations like this within any regional mentality. Of course, you have to remember that today all these traits are much more blurred than they were sixty or seventy years ago.

KRAUSS:

Is Mario von Galli correct when he speaks of Karl Rahner's "grumpy charm"?

RAHNER:

Well, other people must be the judge of that, not I.

KRAUSS:
So you spent your school days in Freiburg and also belonged to a youth group called Fountain of Youth, which you cannot remember in more detail. As a member of that group, you befriended Peter Georgio Frascati. What does this name evoke?

RAHNER:
Around 1920 or 1921, there was an Italian ambassador in Berlin named Frascati. He was a senator and the owner and director of a large Turin newspaper, *La Stampa*. He sent his son, who was a student of mining engineering, to our family to learn German. This young man—he was cheerful and lively and unassuming—he lived with us, not a long time, but still enough for a somewhat lasting relationship to develop, especially with my older sister.

He was, one could say, a very ardent "apostle of charity" in Turin. He died in 1924 of polio contracted in the course of this work, and he is honored in Italy today as a heroic example of a young Christian. It seems that one day he might be beatified in Rome. In a certain way, he was really a strange fellow—athletic, a mountain climber, skier, rider, a funny, happy man who mixed with other students in the liveliest, even wildest way. He told me himself that as a Catholic student in Rome he squabbled with the fascist students from the very beginning.

On the other hand, he was an extraordinarily pious person who prayed, who went to Mass almost every day before the rest of the family got up, and who also displayed extraordinary social concern, as we would call it today, for the poor. It seems he died from this work, eventually contracting polio in this environment. And he thought of the poor until the last hours of his life. Perhaps he will be beatified.

I still remember how enthusiastically he recited Saint Bernard's prayer to Mary from Dante's *Divine Comedy*. Of course, he prayed the rosary in those days. He explained to my mother that he would not become a priest because he thought that in the liberal milieu in which he was born he could do more for the Church and for Christianity religiously as a layman than if he became a priest. On the other hand, he was certainly a man that a girl could love.

I believe that his sister still lives in Rome. She was a Polish diplomat's wife and understood a great deal about her brother's life, precisely because the first biographies were not very good or accurate. They say that the beatification process in Rome—most of the time a long, drawn-out affair—is now gradually coming to a close. If I live to see it, then I would have befriended during my life a beatified person with whom I used to organize wrestling matches in the woods.

ENTRANCE INTO THE
SOCIETY OF JESUS

KRAUSS:
Professor Rahner, in April 1922, three weeks after receiving
your secondary school diploma in Freiburg, you decided to
enter the Society of Jesus. What prompted the then eighteen-
year-old Karl Rahner to become a Jesuit?

RAHNER:
Well, I must say that I actually can't give you any special information about that. Sometime ask an average man, married
some fifty or sixty years, what really prompted him to marry
this particular Maria Meier. If he doesn't fib or hasn't lived a
life of intense self-reflection, he's likely to say: "I completely
admit the fact that I did that. I was faithful to my decision and
was happy throughout the fifty or sixty years of my marriage.
I also accept the fact that normal human motivations prompted
my decision. But I cannot give you any more exact psychological information."

I have to say the same thing about my Jesuit vocation. Obviously I could tell you what might prompt a reasonable young
man to become a priest or a Jesuit, and what it might mean to
assume the priestly ministry in such a tightly knit and organ-
ized society rather than as a diocesan priest. But then these
are all such general and obvious motives that they say very little about my own case.

Of course my brother Hugo, who was four years older, had become a Jesuit in January 1919. He was still a soldier at the end of the First World War, although he was stationed in Belgium and no longer in the real battle. If you ask me what motivated him, then I must admit that I don't exactly know. I do know that he read Moritz Meschler's book, *The Company of Jesus: Their Constitutions and Successes*, as it was called, I think. This impressed him deeply. I don't know the particulars. Alemannian Germans do not speak much about such things, even with brothers they especially like. He became a Jesuit. I would say that that certainly made my decision easier somehow. But I don't attribute great significance to my brother's example for my decision.

I remember now trembling as I shyly informed him—by letter, since he was already in the order, having entered three years ahead of me—that I also wanted to be a Jesuit. I saw him once, I believe, when he was in the novitiate, and also in Valkenburg, Holland, where he studied philosophy. But I would still maintain that this didn't play a direct, decisive role.

KRAUSS:

At that time, around 1922, was the Society of Jesus still somewhat an instrument of the Counter-Reformation? Was there something in the Jesuits that still smacked of the defensive attitude of the Kulturkampf?

RAHNER:

The Jesuits were allowed in Germany again by decree of the Kaiser before the end of the monarchy. But, strictly speaking, we were outlawed from the time of Bismark until 1916 or 1917. Of course, much of that was only on paper. In any case, strictly speaking, we had no houses in Germany so that even the novitiate which I entered was located at Voralberg on Austrian soil. It no longer exists.

But I didn't actually experience a particularly defensive Kulturkampf mentality. Obviously, in those days we Jesuits also shared in the ecclesial Roman Catholic mentality that had evolved in the nineteenth century after the French revolution. Intensified significantly by the Kulturkampf, this mentality became a ghetto mentality—now I don't mean this deprecatingly.

Naturally this mentality also had its variations. But the modern world and the cultural-intellectual life of the rest of German society were still viewed, to some extent at least, with caution, with a certain restraint, and with belligerent rejection. Of course, there were also great variations in this regard.

For example, before the Nazi period, let's say between 1880 and 1930, there were two great Goethe biographies written by Jesuits. One could read these two biographies as paradigms of the development of the ecclesial mentality in which we Jesuits participated. The first biography, by Baumgartner, was, for all its erudition and respect for Goethe, still rather dismissive and critical, emphasizing the unchristian elements in Goethe.

In the twenties, I believe, a shorter but quite spirited biography of Goethe appeared by another Jesuit, Fritz Muckermann. He portrayed Goethe in a much different light. One might say that between 1925 and the Council I lived through a period in which an ecclesiasticism characterized by neoscholasticism and as sharply delimited as possible transformed itself into the Church sanctioned by the Council in which we now live. There were obviously very many sweeping changes. The changes affecting various issues were not synchronized. Thus, some things happened quickly; others slowly. But I would say that if I wanted to classify myself in a cultural-intellectual way, then I belong to this period.

At the start of this period, people like Karl Adam, Peter Lippert, and Erich Przywara had already put a strong stamp on the mentality of German Catholicism. My Jesuit teachers, who came from the old days, would probably have regarded Kant and Hegel and the whole mentality suggested by these names as adversaries.

Later on in the twenties and thirties, interrupted by the Nazi period, open dialogue, mutual instruction, and collaboration were more in evidence. Of course, this also had its dangers. It too can run aground. That must be avoided. But I belonged to this transition period. Keep in mind that I heard the entire corpus of systematic theology at Valkenburg between 1929 and 1933 in Latin!

KRAUSS:
All lectures were in Latin?

RAHNER:
All the lectures were in Latin. The exams were in Latin. The textbooks were in Latin. I myself still lectured in Latin, to some extent at least, here in Innsbruck from 1938 until around 1964. Today no one thinks about that any more. Today no professor could lecture in Latin. Today, even in Rome one couldn't converse in Latin, the Church's Esperanto. But in those days, it was still the case.

FRIENDSHIP
WITH ALFRED DELP

KRAUSS:
During your Jesuit training you taught in Feldkirch/Voralberg from 1927 to 1929. Alfred Delp, who was executed in Berlin as a resistance fighter in February 1945, was one of your students there. What do you remember about him?

RAHNER:
I believe that I can say, with a certain pride (I hope not presumptuously), that Delp and I were good friends. I was the one who had to polish up his Latin in the novitiate. Then we were together for theology in Valkenburg. Even afterwards, our relationship did not break off. When I was working in Vienna, I visited him in Munich shortly before his arrest.

He was a lively and brave person, very much at home in the intellectual atmosphere of his day. He had a certain vitality that did not sit well with his superiors. But he was absolutely faithful and steadfast to his religious order right up to his death, resolutely refusing to be indoctrinated in this regard by his Nazi judges in Berlin.

He was extremely interested in philosophical, sociopolitical, and, if you like, political questions. In fact, he wrote something on Heidegger, the first Catholic book on Heidegger's philosophy. Objectively speaking, it was not very good and has long since been forgotten—and rightly so. But he was true to his ideals and to his vocation, and sealed them with the sacrifice of his life.

He was actually one of the great figures of the so-called Kreisauer circle, the resistance group. He got into this group through Augustin Rösch, the Jesuit Provincial at the time. This group was not involved in planning to assassinate Hitler but in reflecting on what kind of society Germany should become when the dreadful Nazi period finally came to an end. For this, he was arrested and executed. I believe that he really belongs in the front ranks of those witnesses who were motivated by Christianity to resist the evils of Nazism.

KRAUSS:
Do we need martyrs today?

RAHNER:
No one can wish for a period of martyrdom when people are killed for their convictions. But I certainly hope that there are people today who stand unconditionally by their convictions, even at the cost of their lives.

PHILOSOPHICAL STUDIES
IN FREIBURG

Krauss:
Before you could give yourself totally to ecclesial and theological questions, your superiors, to whom you owed obedience, sent you to study philosophy in Freiburg, your hometown. What reputation did the philosophy department at Freiburg have at that time?

Rahner:
Naturally, it had various professors, among them Martin Honecker, who held a chair of Christian philosophy, and also Martin Heidegger, who was already well-known and highly esteemed. We actually enrolled in the theology department because we did not want to spend our time collecting money in a tin cup for "Winter-Aid." That enabled us to sneak off more easily. But we—that means Johann Lotz and I—studied only philosophy, so we participated in Martin Heidegger's seminars for four semesters. And I trust that we learned something from that great philosopher.

Krauss:
Johann Lotz is a fellow Jesuit and one of the leading philosophers of your order today.

RAHNER:

Yes, he worked for years at the Jesuit philosophate in Munich. He often spent semesters teaching philosophy at the Gregorian University in Rome and has written some extraordinarily significant and important things. Both of us entered the Jesuits at approximately the same time, were ordained together in St. Michael's church in Munich by Cardinal Faulhaber in 1932, and also spent four semesters together with Martin Heidegger in Freiburg. I believe Heidegger considered us to be rather good and not completely stupid philosophers.

KRAUSS:

How did it happen that you selected Martin Honecker and not Heidegger as your dissertation director?

RAHNER:

Well, when we came to Freiburg, Martin Heidegger's rather odd and very short university chancellorship at the beginning of the Nazi period had just ended. As young chaplains in clerical black and not Nazi brown, we didn't exactly know how to cope with a Heidegger still linked in some way to Nazism, so we cautiously registered as doctoral students with Martin Honecker. But we were clearly interested in Heidegger's lectures and seminars, and if we had definitely known this right from the beginning, then we could have very easily done our doctoral studies with Heidegger, perhaps even better and more sympathetically as well.

My dissertation director, Martin Honecker, flunked me. Lotz finished his doctoral work under Honecker at the last minute. I was the next one to hand in a dissertation. But I was flunked by the Catholic Honecker for being too inspired by Heidegger. Because I had been reassigned from philosophy to teach theology at Innsbruck, this didn't upset me for long. And I was delighted that I didn't need to minor in Upper Rheinish art history in order to obtain my doctorate in philosophy at Freiburg. My rejected dissertation was then published without my receiving a doctorate; it went through several editions and was translated into many languages. So this failure did not appreciably affect my self-esteem.

KRAUSS:

It is certainly ironic that the philosophy dissertation that Honecker rejected later became, under the title, *Spirit in the World*, a central work in Christian philosophy. Was your stay, your studies, under Honecker merely a fringe episode? Freiburg meant for you studying with Martin Heidegger. At that time, how did one actually get into a Heidegger seminar? It couldn't have been easy.

RAHNER:

A seminar like that was totally different from today's seminars with a hundred or more students crowded together. At that time there were—I no longer remember exactly how many students—but perhaps two dozen at most. And with Heidegger, these were students who had already studied some philosophy. An assistant professor of art history also participated. There were some who later did significant philosophical work.

KRAUSS:

Could you perhaps name a few of Heidegger's students at this time?

RAHNER:

Well, all right. He was no longer in my seminar, but Max Müller was one of Heidegger's students. Gustav Siewerth was another. Then one called Kaliba who was later active in Austria. People of that kind sat in his seminar. You didn't have to take an entrance examination. But Heidegger, in a dignified and critical way, looked over the students who registered for his seminar, asked what they had already studied, and then said: "Yes, that will indeed suffice."

Heidegger used to require us to write up the so-called protocol, minutes of the previous seminar session. These were not long papers or seminar essays, as is usually the case today. But taking those seminar minutes was a rather difficult and ticklish task, because you couldn't simply be a stenographer but had to rework and turn the previous seminar session inside out, and if you then heard Martin Heidegger solemnly say, "The minutes are excellent," you felt as if you had won a medal.

KRAUSS:

When the second edition of *Spirit in the World* appeared in 1957—and the name of Martin Honecker was hardly recognized in Germany—about that time the Martin Heidegger who rarely travelled visited his now famous student, Karl Rahner, at Innsbruck. Do you still remember, Professor Rahner, how the almost seventy-year-old Heidegger affected you? Was there a difference after the long years during which you had not seen each other? Had Heidegger changed?

RAHNER:

Yes, with respect to his philosophy, Heidegger had obviously changed in an extraordinary way, at least in his own view. The later Heidegger who interpreted Nietzsche and published similar works certainly considered himself to be a totally different Heidegger. I must honestly confess that after I became

a theologian and had my own work to do I could no longer
study his thought very extensively. To that extent, I can't
really judge Heidegger's famous reversal.

KRAUSS:
Since Nietzsche, no thinker in Germany has been so enthusiastically acclaimed and, at the same time, so energetically dis-
missed as Martin Heidegger. Some see in him the greatest
philosopher of this century; others consider him a charlatan
and ridicule him as a mystic. How would you judge Heidegger's life and work?

RAHNER:
I would definitely consider him to be a great philosopher.
Other countries, France and North America, studied him and
took him much more seriously than we did. One must distinguish, of course, between what Heidegger meant for his students as a kind of mystagogue in philosophy and what he lectured about in a philosophical and systematic way. For me,
Heidegger's first function was important. He taught us how
to read texts in a new way, to ask what is behind the text, to
see connections between a philosopher's individual texts and
his statements that wouldn't immediately strike the ordinary
person, and so on.

In this way he developed an important philosophy of Being.
That can and will always have a fascinating significance for a
Catholic theologian, for whom God is and remains the inex-
pressible Mystery. If today's positivists, Anglo-Saxon logicians,
and the like have little to say about such things, then, I believe,
this is hardly a justification for minimizing Heidegger's importance. That he never directly and explicitly addressed the actual
question of God as it interests a Catholic theologian is tied up

with his philosophy of Being. It was also perhaps conditioned by Martin Heidegger's personal life, which I cannot go into now. For that reason, I would say that even if he did not expressly raise the God-question in his philosophy of Being, his philosophy is still significant today for Christian theology.

KRAUSS:
What influence did Heidegger's philosophy have on your theological thinking?

RAHNER:
Well, first you must realize that I and Lotz and Max Müller and Bernard Welte and Gustav Siewerth and, later, Emerich Coreth and Otto Muck and other such Christian philosophers had already been influenced, even before reading Heidegger, by the change in traditional Catholic neoscholastic philosophy that had come through the work of the Belgian Jesuit Joseph Maréchal in the 1920s. And to that extent, we were naturally more in tune with Martin Heidegger's thought from the beginning. For that reason, it is difficult to say precisely how much we were influenced by Heidegger, or to say how quickly this turned into, or perhaps returned again to, a more general philosophical, transcendental problematic.

I would say that Heidegger hardly influenced my specifically theological questions, because Heidegger never wrote anything about them. In my manner of thinking, in the courage to question anew so much in the tradition considered self-evident, in the struggle to incorporate modern philosophy into today's Christian theology, here I have certainly learned something from Heidegger and will, therefore, always be thankful to him.

KRAUSS:

At the end of your philosophical studies with Heidegger, you came to Innsbruck in 1936. That same year, very likely toward the end of the year, you wrote your doctoral dissertation in theology. Your brother Hugo had already been appointed professor of early church history and patristics in Innsbruck the previous year. Many things point to your being attracted to your brother's theological field and to your owing him a lot. In retrospect, what would you say about your late brother's work?

RAHNER:

Well, I would say that my brother was a not insignificant patristics scholar, that means an expert in the study of the Church Fathers. He was influenced by Franz-Josef Dölger, under whom he had studied in Bonn. My brother was also a noted scholar in the spirituality of Saint Ignatius of Loyola. He had a certain degree of pastoral interest, too. I believe that I can say that about myself.

For the rest, our theological fields were obviously very different. Of course my doctoral dissertation at Innsbruck handled a patristic theme, for all practical purposes, and to that extent I was certainly much influenced by my brother. But then my philosophical career, if I may say so, and my later work in systematic theology, did not have much to do with him.

There is certainly some connection in the fact that in the 1930s my brother wrote, in addition to his patristic work, a small book on the theology of preaching.* One thought at the time that there must be an immediate connection between

*Hugo Rahner, S.J., *A Theology of Proclamation*, translated by R. Dimler, S.J., W. Dych, S.J., J. Halpin, S.J., and C. Petrick, S.J., adapted by J. Halpin, S.J. (New York: Herder and Herder, 1968).

preaching, proclamation, and theology proper. And so my
brother lectured on and wrote a small theology of preaching
that rather clearly distanced itself from neoscholastic theology.
His theology worked more directly with the Scriptures and
the Fathers. It sought a more immediate relationship to contemporary daily life. And on these points my brother and I
naturally touched base in one way or another. But in other
respects, each of us usually cultivated his own garden and the
immediate connections between us were not so significant.

THE CHURCH UNDER
NATIONAL SOCIALISM

KRAUSS:
Both you and your brother had your teaching activities curtailed when the National Socialists marched into Austria. At that time, you received as it was then called a "district prohibition order." You were no longer allowed to remain in the region. How did it come to that? Why did the National Socialists consider you so dangerous?

RAHNER:
Oh, I suppose that for Gauleiter Hofer, the Nazi district leader of Tyrol, the idea of a Jesuit theological faculty was absolutely intolerable. So he quickly dissolved it. The Canisianum, the seminary for diocesan priests that we ran in Innsbruck, was expropriated. Very soon after, the Jesuit residence for us theology professors was also seized and expropriated. We were thrown out of Innsbruck on short notice. And then we received the district prohibition order. That meant that we were not allowed to stay in the district of Tyrol.

KRAUSS:
You spent the war years in Vienna?

RAHNER:

When we were banished from Innsbruck, I went to Vienna. At the beginning of the war when more and more was being confiscated from our people, we tried to continue teaching theology to Jesuits in Vienna. I worked at the Vienna Pastoral Institute and elsewhere. I was in Vienna until the summer of 1944. Then I went to Lower Bavaria during the vacation period and didn't return to Vienna but spent the last year of the war in Lower Bavaria.

KRAUSS:

Can one say that the Austrian Catholic Church offered more resistance to National Socialism than the German?

RAHNER:

The German Jesuits?

KRAUSS:

The German dioceses.

RAHNER:

Well, I don't believe that. It was probably more or less the same in Austria and in Germany. Resistance could have been greater and more explicit, but National Socialism actually had no friends among church communities, religious orders, priests, and bishops. Delp wasn't the only one who was killed by the Nazis. There is an entire list of other Jesuits, both German and Austrian, who were executed under National Socialism.

KRAUSS:

In your opinion, to what extent should the Vatican have more clearly defended itself against National Socialism?

RAHNER:

That is a question that I really can't answer. Naturally, more explicit, more dramatic, more public opposition would have been desirable. Why didn't Pope Pius XII do that? Did he hope to accomplish more by other means? Was such a view justified? In retrospect, who can say? To mount attacks like Hochhuth's *The Deputy* seems to me more or less unjust.

I really cannot explain historically, philosophically, and sociopolitically the phenomenon of National Socialism and the pathos with which this horror so patently manifested itself and ruled every dimension of public life. Times of collective madness like this are basically unexplainable. If you keep in mind that I knew many people whose personal and moral integrity I can't call into question in any way yet who still believed after a long time or well into the war that National Socialism was a real blessing for the German people— and, on the other hand, if one asks oneself critically if one wasn't a clear opponent of Nazism simply because as a Catholic priest one was excluded a priori from the Nazi party, and also because the Nazi party so vehemently attacked one's Christian convictions—then, when all is said and done, one really doesn't know, even in hindsight, what one should have done at the time. One doesn't even know what one did right or wrong during that period.

Naturally, one can always say in retrospect that one acted cowardly, and perhaps such a judgment is justified, too. But I would still say to today's youth: Try living in such times! I hope you never have to! And if you too must go through the times we did, then let's see if you will be that much more prescient, courageous, and willing to risk your lives than we were in our time.

KRAUSS:

If a contemporary student asked you how you would explain the Hitler phenomenon, his overwhelming power, what would you say in response?

RAHNER:

I would say: "My dear friend, naturally I can list all the possible reasons—cultural, historical, economic, and the like. I can even give reasons that no longer contain the danger of Nazism in the usual sense because they no longer exist today. But I cannot explain to you the 'Hitler phenomenon.'" How such a primitive man could have attracted and swayed people whose character and morality I simply cannot deny still puzzles me today.

I was not one of those people. But I can't praise myself for that, since, as I've said, from the start National Socialism was not an option to which a Roman Catholic priest could give his assent—and this was mutually understood. But this clear opposition to Nazism was so socially pre-programmed that I cannot take any credit for it. At most, one can ask oneself: Why didn't you protest much more clearly and plainly?

Of course I knew people in Vienna who had to go about wearing the star of David. I had contact with people, Jesuits as well, who placed themselves in grave danger to care for Jews. But by and large, it is still true that we endured this madness rather passively. In retrospect, we must ask ourselves what we in fact should have done. An Alfred Delp, a Rösch, a Father Grimm, and many others actively fought in their small groups against the Nazis. Even bishops like Gröber, who thought at first in his well-meaning fashion that he could meet Nazism half-way, wound up preaching boldly against the Nazis in the last years of the war. And don't forget Cardinal von Galen.

But how should one have actually behaved, worked, protested, and taken to the barricades in those days? That I don't know even today.

KRAUSS:
During the time you were in Vienna, the so-called Vienna memorandum originated. What was it all about?

RAHNER:
Well, the good archbishop of Freiburg, Konrad Gröber, had the strange idea of protesting certain ecclesial—not political—tendencies. In a memorandum, a letter to the Greater German episcopacy, as he called it, he expressed observations and fears concerning certain tendencies in liturgy, in current theology, and in pastoral practices. And I received at this time a commission from Cardinal Innitzer, and from the Vienna Pastoral Institute directed by Karl Rudolph, to draw up a counter-memorandum. And I did so.

In retrospect, one has heard little about either memorandum. The German bishops had concerns other than Konrad Gröber's, and after the war, when Germany and Austria were divided, there was no more talk about it. A biography of Konrad Gröber, published a short while ago, gives a certain historical account of the entire matter. The book blurs the issues a bit and renders the affair somewhat insignificant. Still, one can read there what significance the Vienna memorandum had for this period of history.

KRAUSS:
Could one say that, for all practical purposes, Lefebvre and his followers today raise the same points of contention that Archbishop Konrad Gröber raised in 1943?

RAHNER:

One could perhaps detect and show a certain parallel. However, Konrad Gröber was a German who grew up in Rome, and as one so obviously loyal to Rome, he would have never come upon the idea of protesting the Second Vatican Council, as Lefebvre has done.

KRAUSS:

At that time, therefore, the Greater German episcopacy attributed little significance to Gröber's letter of accusation?

RAHNER:

I have never noticed anything about it having particular importance.

FROM THE END OF WORLD WAR II
TO VATICAN COUNCIL II

KRAUSS:
In your rejoinder to Gröber's letter of accusation, you offered the sober diagnosis, perhaps one could better say, the demand, that Catholic theology begin its scientific encounter with the problems of the contemporary world. Can one say that the teaching activity that you resumed here in Innsbruck after the war had precisely this as its point of departure?

RAHNER:
One can say that. One can also quite soberly ask: What else should a Catholic theologian do, if he does his work? Naturally, one can do theology as it was done before the Second World War. Think about how Grabmann, Landgraf, Pelster, Ehrle, and others buried themselves in the history of medieval theology. For them, it was as if the development that Catholic theology had undergone from the Middle Ages through the baroque era right up to the neoscholastic period of the nineteenth century could no longer seriously continue.

Landgraf, who was an important researcher of the early scholasticism of the Middle Ages, was possibly convinced that such a high point had been reached in systematic theology that one could actually never surpass it. In this respect we have more recent theologians—whom I do not need to enumerate and among whom I played a modest role—who had a hand in bringing about a considerable change in theology. So much so that today one could even say that historical theology is being grudgingly revised, but I don't know. However, I do know that an incredible change of mentality took place in Catholic theology in the 1940s and 1950s. Of course, biblical exegesis attained a totally different ranking than it had in neo-scholastic theology.

KRAUSS:

How would you define more exactly your theological point of departure? Is it correct that your theology does not proceed from handy dogmas that are simply to be believed but begins with the current situation of the contemporary person?

RAHNER:

I would not consider these alternatives justified. As a Catholic theologian, I cannot at any point in my considerations, in my thinking, in my work, *not* take into account the question: "What does the magisterium, the ecclesial teaching office, teach about this or that question"? Still, I can't simply be a parrot. I must reflect upon what a particular church teaching actually means, what its actual purpose is, into which context I must place it so that it is really, personally, and genuinely accepted. And along with such necessary questions, the cultural-intellectual situation of one's own day is certainly an indispensable milieu within which theology must be done.

And I must further respond: What can I say as a Catholic theologian about the doctrines of the world's beginnings and creation, if I take into account without bias the results of modern physics and paleontology? We would certainly have somewhat suppressed these and similar questions in the nineteenth century. But we cannot afford to do that today. And as much as I am able, I want to avoid the danger of theologizing in a self-enclosed Catholic ghetto. How far I have succeeded is another question.

KRAUSS:
Professor Rahner, doesn't your theology have its own special brand of rationality?

RAHNER:
I would say that in theology as well as anywhere else one cannot think enough, think intensively enough, courageously enough, and precisely enough. And if you want to call this "rational," then I completely agree that my theology is rational. I would also say that if Catholic theology is to be a theology of the incomprehensible God, then it must obviously reckon with mystery. But in too many cases, traditional theology said that mystery began where it could have and should have thought more profoundly. Too often it simply ascribed particular questions to mystery, whereas the true mystagogical character of theology must lead it into the presence of the one, same, and only all-embracing mystery of God.

KRAUSS:
Can one say that your theology begins where textbook theology ends?

RAHNER:
You know, even the theology of the schools really said the most important things. But often the school theologians did not sufficiently bear in mind what colossal, mysterious, and personally radical things their theses actually said, the theses

they propounded so casually and harmlessly. It is not as if you could discover something totally new in Catholic theology, something our forefathers had not thought of or said in their own theology.

The thesis that God is incomprehensible was always present in Catholic theology. For Thomas Aquinas, something like that was self-evident. For Thomas Aquinas, it was also self-evident that God, even in the so-called immediate vision of God in eternity, still remains the incomprehensible, unfathomable mystery. But a contemporary theology could place such a thesis much more radically, I might add, at the center of the theological enterprise. And from this center, all other theological statements receive yet another color and shading. Therefore, there is something like a controlling center for theology.

You may say that I have indeed said nothing that has not been said before. I would even consider that a plus for my theology and by no means a negative judgment. But you can also say that from me, but not only from me, the whole of theology takes on a new appearance.

KRAUSS:
Professor Rahner, can one say that your life, your biography, hasn't been very exciting? Rather, your bibliography, with its numerous subtle essays both on theological-philosophical problems and on the truisms of the everyday life of the Church and of the individual Christian, is much more dramatic?

RAHNER:
My friend Johann Baptist Metz once told me that my biography is identical with my theology. Perhaps one can say that. Indeed, I lived through the First World War, through

Karl Rahner's parents, Luise (1868-1976) and Karl (1875-1934). Photo: Karl-Rahner-Archiv, Innsbruck

As a two-year-old *(center)* on Shrove Tuesday, 1906, with *(left to right)* sister Anna, brothers Georg and Hugo, and a cousin. Photo: Karl Rahner-Archiv, Insbruck.

Toasting his mother on her hundredth birthday with Theophil Herder-Dorneich, publisher of Herder Verlag. Photo: (Alber-) Bildverlag, Freiburg

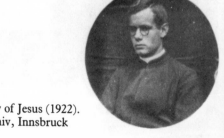

As a novice in the Society of Jesus (1922).
Photo: Karl-Rahner-Archiv, Innsbruck

the Second World War, and through the perils of the Nazi period. I was, if you will, exiled. I did not have much to eat in the last war and so on. In a certain sense, then, I can be reckoned among those ordinary people who survived those times. Still, I was certainly one of those spared the most frightening horrors of those days.

KRAUSS:

Can one say, therefore, that your bibliography is more dramatic than your biography?

RAHNER:

Yes, yes, one can. If the bibliography can be called dramatic—of course, that is another question!—certainly! My personal life took place essentially—obviously, not only!—in theological work.

KRAUSS:

Your thinking did not produce a large textbook but numerous individual articles that came to comprise fifteen German volumes, with the sixteenth in progress, of *Schriften zur Theologie*. Why hasn't Professor Rahner written a systematic theology textbook, a dogmatic theology in the strict sense?

RAHNER:

That is not easy to answer. First, let me point out that I did write a sort of summary of my theology a few years back in the book entitled *Foundations of Christian Faith: An Introduction to the Idea of Christianity*.* These several hundred pages do contain, to some extent, a summary of my theology.

By and large, it is true that I produced a mass of separate theological investigations in individual essays. On the one

*Translated by William V. Dych (New York: Crossroad, 1978).

hand, this is simply because of the time required of a person to do individual investigations step by step and case by case. On the other hand, perhaps a systematic, architechtonic theology, as envisioned in earlier times, can no longer be done by a single theologian.

I coproduced the large, multivolume *Mysterium Salutis*. But that project required the cooperation of many people. Today if you wish to work on any topic in systematic theology, you naturally have to pay very close attention to the history of dogma, exegesis, and the like, much more than a theologian did in the neoscholastic period right up to the middle of the twentieth century. Hence, this is a task that obviously exceeds what one person can do alone.

KRAUSS:

Is your "lack of a system" only something that originates by chance from your individual psychology and biography? Or isn't there still basically a system to be found in your theology and even more than one would at first suspect?

RAHNER:

Well, I've already said that I've always held the opinion that one must think systematically in theology as well as anywhere else. I believe that I am one of those theologians who, if I remember correctly, defended the thesis that theology must be able to compress itself again and again into so-called basic formulas of faith. And I want to say that one must be able to express, in almost a few sentences, what actually constitutes the essence of Christianity. I said that as normative as the Apostles' Creed will remain for Christians in the future, still other basic formulas must be found that might be more intelligible and more immediately meaningful to a person today or in the next century than such old creedal formulas.

KRAUSS:

Professor Rahner, in surveying the fullness of your literary accomplishments—which is after all almost impossible—the question arises how you accomplished all that in addition to your numerous other obligations, and on top of that when one hears you say, and I quote you: "There are days when I write nothing!"

RAHNER:

You see, I've always gone to bed early and gotten up relatively early. I've had few hobbies. I was neither a mountain climber nor a photographer, nor did I lead an intense social life. So if you spend your days in a certain eremetical way of life, then you don't need to get up very early or work late at night, and if God gives you the opportunity, you can work calm and undisturbed, and very easily do the work that I did. This has not been so tragic.

KRAUSS:
So, you have no hobbies?

RAHNER:
Well, I don't know about no hobbies at all. For many years I smoked, beginning with my bee-keeping days in Valkenburg. But other than that, I don't know what particular hobbies I've had. Many scholars, in addition to their professional work, happen to have some other interests. A biochemist like Eichen is an important musician to this day. Maier-Leibnitz, the physicist, published a cookbook, didn't he? Some people can do that. It is splendid and admirable. But I didn't go to the theater often because my hearing was not good. Actually I don't have a very intense, personal interest in music. I'm ashamed to admit it. But if a person accepts himself as he is and takes

satisfaction in what he can do, then the quantity of what he does is no particular problem.

KRAUSS:

It is all the more astonishing to me that you have, if not a relationship, then at least some contact with the authors of our day. Take Heinrich Böll or Luise Rinser. How do you judge their work?

RAHNER:

Heinrich Böll has been rather kind to me. Apparently because he did not consider me exactly a church-conformist in my thinking. I also know Luise Rinser, due to certain connections that developed at the Council. Of course, I know my colleagues in the Order of Merit. All branches of science and culture are represented there.

To that extent I couldn't say that I've been a theological Carthusian living in a cloistered monastery where one notices nothing of the world. I only wanted to clarify why the question how I accomplished all I did is in fact not a very pressing one, requiring explanation and clarification. My work came of itself.

A THEOLOGIAN
WITH A MIND OF HIS OWN

KRAUSS:
Church officials were not always pleased with what you said
and wrote about God, the world, and the Church. How did
you react to this experience?

RAHNER:
First of all, I would say that all the things that happened did
not affect me as terribly as they might affect young theologians
today. You see, if a person is a member of a religious order, a
Jesuit, and really takes into account the fact that his religious
superior can send him to India or to the African bush—and
that this can happen without further ado—then one does not
get so frightfully worked up about getting into occasional difficulties with Rome over one's theological work.

When the Congregation of Faith in Rome under Cardinal
Ottaviani once said that I could write only in conjunction
with a special Roman censor, then I said to myself: "Well, I
just won't write anymore, and then the matter is over and
done with, right?" But nothing came of it because the Council
arrived. And according to Roman methods, such instructions
are then silently forgotten. But you see from this that in the
old days a Catholic theologian didn't get as worked up about
this sort of thing as one does today.

KRAUSS:

So you were once canonically forbidden to write, even if this was long ago rescinded?

RAHNER:

The main thing was that I was partially silenced by Rome. But that also was withdrawn. And Rome once sent someone to Innsbruck to make inquiries on the spot as to how I actually did theology, but he was very friendly, very fair, and objective, and did me no harm. And I once had this special Roman censor, but nothing practical or concrete ever came of it.

KRAUSS:

At that time, Cardinal Ottaviani was responsible for all this. What kind of a person was he?

RAHNER:

Ottaviani was a Roman canonist, a church lawyer. At that time he directed the Holy Office, now called the Congregation for the Doctrine of the Faith. He styled himself a watchdog of the Holy See. Naturally, he had a somewhat old-fashioned theology, which he regarded as self-evident. Hence, he objected to this and that in my theology.

But personally he was actually a splendid fellow. He founded or directed an orphanage on his own initiative. He was personally very nice. He once took me in his Mercedes from Innsbruck to Munich for a eucharistic congress. We said the rosary in Latin together and didn't discuss church politics at all. During the Council, when he was the head of the theological commission for the Council to which I belonged as a "peritus," he once said to me: "Well, we have absolutely nothing against you. You see, this extraordinary Roman censor is a special

privilege by which we wish to protect you from the misunderstandings of dumb friends." Then I said: "Your Eminence, I
renounce privileges." And since then, there hasn't actually
been anything more.

They even invited me to visit the old, retired prefect of the
Congregation, but I didn't go. In the old days one experienced
and interpreted these things differently, even in the Congregation itself. Perhaps at the time they considered me a rash
and wild theologian who needed his knuckles rapped. But that
had nothing at all to do with personal animosity or the like.
To be sure, certain things did happen that absolutely shouldn't
have.

KRAUSS:
For example?

RAHNER:
I mean, for instance, when a German theologian learned from
the newspapers that one of his books was on the Index—the
list of books forbidden by the Church. That was just plain
inexcusable.

KRAUSS:
You speak of Küng?

RAHNER:
No, this was much earlier. He was a theologian in Trier, but
his name escapes me.

KRAUSS:
But the same thing happened to Küng, didn't it?

RAHNER:

No—Küng, that was a very intricate process. Whether it came to a just conclusion, I don't quite know. But things happened time and again that as far as the Romans are concerned are more or less self-evident practices and ways of looking at things. They are things that I have absolutely no wish to defend when I say that I did not personally feel so terribly persecuted. You've got to distinguish between how an old-style theologian like myself experiences things like that and the totally different question of how the objective procedures of the Congregation of Faith ought to be conducted: They must be just, therefore objective, and the greatest stupidities must not be allowed to occur.

KRAUSS:

But doesn't that happen on occasion? Do you believe that this institution, the Congregation of Faith, is still necessary today?

RAHNER:

Certainly. Consequently, I would absolutely affirm the essential function of the Congregation of Faith even today. However, it is still another question how this task is to be accomplished, whether petty censures should be imposed, and whether the Congregation of Faith ought not to work in a much more positive manner. But I believe that even in the Protestant churches there can and should be something like disciplinary procedures on matters of church teaching. Therefore, in no way do I dispute the basic justification for such an institution. In certain circumstances, there are bound to be intramural squabbles. I myself was once the defender, the defense expert, so to speak, in a session of the Congregation of Faith that dealt with Edward Schillebeeckx, the Dutch theologian.

KRAUSS:
How had he given Rome offence?

RAHNER:
On various grounds. Christology, I believe. But other things as well. There was a full docket of serious objections against him. But at least the matter was dropped.

KRAUSS:
Professor Rahner, you said once: "Even a definitively binding dogma proclaimed by the Church is essentially open to the future. A dogma must always be interpreted anew to remain alive, and this always permits even diverse interpretive possibilities in the contemporary situation."

Such a statement from your lips may indeed help the faith of some people; for others, it may be rather a hindrance to faith, because it could lead to error, perhaps even to disturbing the faith. Does it bother you that your statements are indeed a help to faith for some, but for others are more of an obstacle to faith?

RAHNER:
Well, show me the theologian in the whole history of the Church of whom this was not unavoidably the case. The bishop of Paris objected to the saintly Thomas Aquinas. Obviously, Aquinas's theology unsettled him. And so with Suarez, the great baroque theologian of the Jesuit order—he also had troubles with Rome. Things like this cannot be avoided. It is self-evident to me that a dogma ought not to be distorted or denied in its real, originally intended meaning. But it is also self-evident that through new theological effort, every dogma can always be thought through anew, made new, and consid-

ered in other connections, and so to that extent every dogma is open to the future. That is something self-evident.

KRAUSS:
For you?

RAHNER:
For normal Catholic theology—because one can prove rather easily from church history that even the Church's teaching office, in certain circumstances, revised its earlier statements, and interpreted them anew. Consequently, what is fair for the Roman teaching office is obviously permitted to the average theologian too within the limits of his duties.

IS THERE A
"CHRISTIAN" CONSCIENCE?

KRAUSS:

There are Christians, you've once said, to whom you attribute a good conscience for actions in the moral area that your own conscience, however, would reject in certain circumstances. Concretely: A Christian family—and the emphasis is on "Christian"—a Christian family decides to obtain an abortion for reasons that may be unclear to an outsider. If you yourself reject a medical procedure like abortion on the grounds that your conscience does not permit it, do you allow fellow Christians to hold another opinion? Do you allow this without denying their Christianity? Or without saying: "A Christian who does that is guilty"?

RAHNER:

To begin with, it is perfectly clear that there are different opinions about very important matters depending upon the circumstances, even in orthodox Catholic moral theology. Hence, it is already obvious that Catholic moral theology allows a person in "good faith," that means with a good conscience, to decide, without guilt before God, something that a moral theologian judges as objectively false. Moreover, it is clearly self-evident that a distinction can always be made between the objective norm and what an individual subjective

69

conscience considers right. And to that extent, I can certainly concede that in many cases another Christian in his conscience before God may consider something as morally permitted that I or another theologian or even the official teaching of the Church declares as objectively contravening God's norms.

KRAUSS:

Shouldn't that be publicized more? Shouldn't it become much more widely known that even a Catholic can act absolutely according to his conscience and not be bound by doctrines and decrees that come from bishops or even from Rome?

RAHNER:

No, I believe that's an incorrect way of posing the question. Every subjective conscience is obliged to do everything in its power to conform to objective norms, according to the objective facts of a moral situation. Consequently, a subjective conscience is clearly required in principle to conform to the Church's moral teaching. But there are obviously cases in which an individual conscience can imagine it could legitimately depart from the official norm in this or that particular case, cases that are theoretically not quite so predictable.

KRAUSS:

Is there a Christian conscience?

RAHNER:

Of course! There is a Christian conscience directed by God's revelation in Jesus Christ and in Holy Scripture. A Christian conscience is a conscience that knows itself to be bound in principle to the revelation of God in Jesus Christ, as it is given in Scripture and Tradition.

KRAUSS:
Professor Rahner, does it annoy you that many of your statements are disposed of—from whatever quarter—as the grumblings of an old man?

RAHNER:
I suppose that every theologian faces the unavoidable fate of growing old, of no longer standing in the forefront of the theological enterprise, of having younger people get the impression that he has gotten old, that he is perhaps old-fashioned or more reactionary than he was when he was young. That is a normal consequence of old age. One shouldn't let oneself get worked up about it.

The fact is simply that the "old-fashioned" opinion or view or teaching can be right and the newer one wrong. In such matters, one shouldn't fret over public opinion but ask: "How is the matter to be judged concretely? In this particular instance, is the newer or the older attitude or opinion the right one?"

KRAUSS:
Therefore, with no preconceived notions, but . . .

RAHNER:
No. Not everything new is good, and not everything old is bad, and neither is everything new bad and everything old good! One must always examine each case with fresh eyes.

KRAUSS:
In this context, I think about Rainer Maria Rilke's words: "A man's reputation is the sum of the public misunderstandings about him." Are these words true of you?

RAHNER:

I believe that Rilke said more intelligent and more profound things than that. It can certainly happen that much about a person may be misunderstood, may be too quickly interpreted away, and so on, and that part of one's reputation rests on such misunderstandings. But I trust that, by and large, this is not true of my modest theology. I believe that many people have understood my theology and have also put it into practice.

If I might tell this story. I once said to Paul VI in a private audience: "You know, Holy Father, a few years ago the Holy Office forbade me to publish anything new on concelebration. Today you yourself concelebrate." He smiled gently and said: "Yes, there is a time for laughing and a time for crying." What he really meant in this context, I don't know. But you see from this little anecdote that it is impossible to say that everything said is said in vain, or that only misunderstandings of what one says have a future.

ROMANO GUARDINI'S
SUCCESSOR

KRAUSS:

Professor Rahner, after fifteen years of teaching at Innsbruck, you were called in 1964 to be Romano Guardini's successor in Munich in the academic chair for Christian philosophy and the philosophy of religion. What did that succession mean to you?

RAHNER:

I certainly felt it was something very appealing and quite an honor, because this appointment came ultimately from Romano Guardini himself. I discussed it with him beforehand, and I gladly accepted it, even though later much happened other than originally planned. I had always held Guardini in high esteem, and for that reason this appointment was something significant, something different, for example, from an earlier experience when on the order of my religious superiors I immediately had to refuse a possible appointment to Münster. My superiors did not want me to leave Innsbruck for Münster before 1964, because they claimed to need me there, but they readily allowed me to go to Munich.

KRAUSS:

What was the special timbre of Romano Guardini's personality?

RAHNER:

Let me start with one of his own remarks. He once said that as a young theologian he had been traumatized during the period of modernism and antimodernism under Pius X, and that he never completely got over it. Without a doubt, as a theologian Guardini wished to be at peace with the Church and with the Roman magisterium, and because he believed that as a young theologian he had had very bad experiences with Rome during the modernist period, that is around 1910, he avoided the possibility of conflict right from the start, in my estimation, by the kinds of questions he selected in his theological work.

For that reason he was primarily a philosopher of religion, one who describes religious phenomena with great insight and patience. And he accomplished extraordinary things in that field in his dialogues with modern literature, whether with Raabe, Dostoyevsky, Rilke, or the like. Yet in one way or another he always anxiously avoided questions in dogmatic and systematic theology. Perhaps his whole mentality and ability did lean in the other direction, although his doctoral dissertation and his first postdoctoral work actually moved more in the direction of theology. But he did not do that.

KRAUSS:

May I ask again why you nevertheless left Munich after a relatively short time to go to Münster, where you were professor of dogmatics and the history of dogma until you became emeritus in 1971?

RAHNER:

Well, I really want to talk about this honestly. I hope that I don't tread too heavily on anyone's toes in Munich. It was simply this way: I received a call to Münster, and with the approval of the Minister of Education at the time and of Cardinal Döpfner, I said: "I'll stay in Munich if I'm allowed to have doctoral students." That was because I wanted an assistant and co-workers who would receive doctorates in theology and then could advance academically in this field.

KRAUSS:
And that was not possible in Munich?

RAHNER:
For all practical purposes the theology faculty refused me this rather harmless and in other respects obvious and common enough request. Then the only thing I could really say was: "Good, then I'll accept the appointment to Münster." Guardini was very disappointed in me and vexed about the matter. Still, there was really nothing else I could do.

THEOLOGY IN DIALOGUE
WITH THE CONTEMPORARY WORLD

KRAUSS:

Your theological output, Professor Rahner, is distinguished by an incredible variety of themes, a richness of thinking, and an astonishing breadth. I'm thinking here about your efforts to bring theology and science into dialogue, or to rethink the relationship of Christianity to non-Christian religions. Yes, even to seeking dialogue with atheism and Marxism. With respect to all these unified themes, I am eager to ask you something. In your view, are there limits for the scientist? Is there a boundary that should not be crossed? For example, take genetic research.

RAHNER:

Well, I think that one must certainly make a distinction between science as science and the practical application of scientific knowledge. If you engage in atomic physics, then you can build an atomic bomb, and the question becomes whether you should use your perfectly legitimate scientific knowledge to construct atomic bombs. That you should scientifically engage in fission research and things like that is obvious. You can pursue the study of human genetics as a science. That is one

side of the question. Whether you should pursue this in practice as well, on humane and moral grounds, is another. You
can create test-tube babies. You can effect genetic manipula-
tion. The question is whether this is reasonable, whether it is
right.

KRAUSS:
Are there limits from a Christian perspective that must be ob-
served, limits that should not be crossed?

RAHNER:
I would say that where something becomes inhumane, inhu-
man, and basically violates the dignity of the spiritual person,
then it ceases to be meaningful and good. When and where
that occurs must obviously be considered on a case-to-case
basis. Clearly, on this point there can also be differences of
opinion. But I am not competent to go into that.

KRAUSS:
A few years ago your definition of anonymous Christianity
caused quite a stir. What does it really mean?

RAHNER:
You see, what it means is terribly simple and straightforward.
Whether one should use the label "anonymous Christianity"
or not is something one can argue about. What is meant is
that someone who follows his own conscience, whether he
thinks he should be a Christian or not, whether he thinks he
should be an atheist or not, is accepted before God and by
God, and can reach that eternal life we confess in our Christian faith as the goal of all. In other words, grace and justification, relationship and union with God, and the possibility of

attaining eternal life are only limited by a person's bad conscience. And that is in fact what the term "anonymous Christianity" tries to say.

KRAUSS:

Isn't that a strangely liberal thesis for a Catholic theologian?

RAHNER:

No. One cannot say that. Consider the fact that the notion of baptism of desire, as it is called, was around at the Council of Trent, that is, centuries ago. This theory, according to old Catholic teaching that goes back to Saint Ambrose, holds that someone whose moral inclinations are actually oriented toward God is already justified even if he or she hasn't been baptized yet.

KRAUSS:

Doesn't this definition of anonymous Christianity put Christianity's absolute claim in jeopardy?

RAHNER:

In order to maintain Christianity's absolute claim (and a thoroughly justified claim at that) and to reconcile the notion of anonymous Christianity with all that is said in the New Testament about the necessity of baptism and Christian faith, one must obviously do some thinking. But one can do that. One can maintain Christianity's claim to be the culmination of the graced relationship of humanity to God both verbally and institutionally without in any way denying the teaching that anyone who does not lock God out by real, personal, deadly guilt is safe in God's love and in His salvation.

KRAUSS:

I'd like to ask you a question about your efforts to dialogue with atheists and Marxists. Is Christianity partially responsible for the rise of contemporary atheism?

RAHNER:

Perhaps if one is willing to think very deeply, one can positively show that Christianity legitimately undertook, we can say, a denuminization of the world, a secularization of the world no longer considered divine. In this way, Christianity paved the way for the possibility of a more powerful atheism to affect human consciousness than had previously been the case. But for that very reason, Christianity is nevertheless quite correct in its confession of the living, eternal God who is totally different from, yet radically immanent to, all dimensions of the world. Atheism is a horrible deformation of the person and of human consciousness.

KRAUSS:

Can it be said that although Marxism and Christianity do not have common starting points, they still have a common goal?

RAHNER:

Of course, there always exists among all people an ultimate togetherness, even with respect to the future. However, where communism means dialectical materialism, and where it is made into a state religion, it is certainly totally unacceptable for a Christian. It is a completely different question whether Christians cannot and should not be more open, more active, and less prejudiced in discussing with Marxists possible structures for a more humane society and economy, for social and economic change. That, I think, is a totally different question.

But a state Marxism, if I can call it that, that elevates atheism to a state religion and that tolerates Christians only on the fringes of its life, is unacceptable to us. If we are Christians and want to remain Christians, that seems self-evident to me.

KRAUSS:
Therefore, you see no parallels. Can't one at least say that Christianity and Marxism pursue the same goal?

RAHNER:
I would not say "the same goal." For if the ultimate goal is different for both of us—and there can be no doubt about that—there can of course be certain routes on which some paths have relatively similar and parallel stretches. But the difference in the ultimate goal also makes itself felt in the stretches of road that are not even close to the ultimate goal. One can see this, of course, in the actual conduct of a Christian statesman and of one who is simply a Marxist.

That there are many things in which we can be united with Marxists cannot be doubted, even after what I've just said. That the poor must be treated more decently, that they should not be oppressed, that terrible social conditions exist in Latin America, about these and similar things Christians and Marxists know themselves in fact to be united. Where the poor are exploited, a Marxist and a Christian must obviously join together to fight such exploitation.

THE SECOND
VATICAN COUNCIL

KRAUSS:

Professor Rahner, the highpoint of your accomplishments can certainly be seen in the fact that you were one of the most significant, internationally renowned key figures of the Second Vatican Council.

RAHNER:

Not really. I think that's an exaggeration. Yes, I was present at the Second Vatican Council. I also had contact with German and Austrian bishops. The Brazilian bishops invited me to speak several times. Once I was with the Polish bishops. I was a member of the theological commission that produced both the decree on the Church and the one on divine revelation, and I was on the commission that wrote the document on the relationship of the Church to the modern world.

But by the very nature of things, there were a lot of cooks at the Second Vatican Council, lots of co-workers, theologians, and bishops. If you keep in mind that two thousand bishops suggested hundreds and hundreds of changes for every decree, and that I certainly wasn't the boss of the theological commission or of the theologians, let alone the bishops, then you won't regard me as if I held a key position at the Second Vatican Council. There were a number of different decrees. For the most part, I learned something about most of them only after they had long been completed and approved.

KRAUSS:
Your great modesty shows itself again. The fact remains that you had a hand in the final corrections.

RAHNER:
No, no, no!

KRAUSS:
Still, it was no accident that the cardinals called you the "Holy Ghost Writer" of the Council.

RAHNER:
Well, that's nonsense, isn't it? Naturally I did my share. One could say that if certain theologians, and not only I, had not had a good working relationship with the bishops at the start of the Council, perhaps, humanly speaking, the die would have been cast quite differently from the way it actually was. You see, there was an incredible number of so-called schemata, texts prepared ahead of time by Roman theologians. These Roman theologians had the notion that the bishops had come to Rome only to applaud their ready-made texts, and that the Council could then adjourn after a few days.

In fact, as it happened, not one of the preconciliar drafts came up for debate during the Council at all. The die had obviously been cast even more decisively, not by the theologians now, but by Suenens, Döpfner, and other cardinals. The theologians, too, had an important hand in bringing about the mentality that ensued. Clearly it is no longer possible to give you detailed, concrete proof of this. That is true. Still, at the time, Ratzinger, Schillebeeckx, Semmelroth, Grillmeier, and their kind were the theologians who were especially important for creating the right ambience at the beginning of the Council. But once the die was cast, we theologians, not only I but many others, worked together on the details honestly and sensibly. But at the time, I did not play an especially exciting role.

KRAUSS:

You mentioned that you belonged to the papal and episcopal theological commissions, and also played the role of mediator between the hierarchy and the people of God. Professor Rahner, where did you get your ecclesially independent authority which was not only striking when you were an adviser at the Council but still impresses anyone who knows you?

RAHNER:

I was a member of the papal international theological commission for a while, but then I quit because it bored me and struck me as too inefficient. I was on the theological commission for the German bishops' conference for a time, too. When you say that I had an authority independent of these official authorities—and I don't rightly know how great this authority really is—well, if it exists and to the extent that it exists, it comes, I would say, from my attempt to argue cogently regarding whatever matter is at hand. One cannot do more than that. Besides, I haven't completely avoided being a bit courageous in church affairs.

KRAUSS:

What would you have wanted to be different in these commissions?

RAHNER:

Well, I would have wanted the international theological commission to be seriously consulted on questions concretely relevant to the Congregation of Faith. The prefect for the Congregation of Faith at the time, the now deceased Cardinal Seper, had clearly not wanted this. So the Roman commission ended up being a theologians' club where intelligent theologians intelligently dialogued with one another. Still, I had the impression that I didn't need to go to Rome for that. I can do that just as well with my colleagues in Germany. And in Germany the results are more or less the same as they are in this Roman theological commission. So, why should I travel to Rome? Right? I can eat ice cream in Germany too, although the ice cream in Rome is excellent.

KRAUSS:

Did you sometimes eat ice cream in Rome?

RAHNER:

Yes, yes, and I can recommend to you a very good ice cream stand on the Piazza Navona.

KRAUSS:

So you too occasionally enjoy the good things in life?

RAHNER:

Certainly, and why not? One of our Jesuit ascetics said some sixty or seventy years ago: "The good things in life are not only for the rascals!"

KRAUSS:

When John XXIII announced the Second Vatican Council on January 25, 1959, what were your thoughts when you first heard about it?

RAHNER:

I don't exactly remember any more. I know, or at least I know in retrospect, that an influential adviser to Pius XII, a moral theologian at the Gregorian, the Pontifical University, refused to recommend my appointment as an adviser to the Council. Many in Rome didn't hold me in very high regard. Still, an appointment to the preconciliar commission did come relatively soon, apparently ordered by John XXIII. That was only a gesture, because, for all practical purposes, I was never invited to Rome for any of the sessions of this commission.

But it did break the ice somewhat. From the beginning, I was a peritus, that is, a theological adviser at the Second Vatican Council. Cardinal König took me along to Rome as his adviser, and he saw to it from the outset that I join the theological commission, which wasn't in itself a foregone conclusion. There were quite a few periti in Rome during the Council who were only there, to put it crudely, to stand around or to occupy themselves with extraconciliar business. And it didn't just happen that one simply got onto a particular conciliar commission without more ado.

I believe it was Cardinal König who encouraged me to get onto the theological commission, and it also happened that Cardinal Ottaviani did not throw me out—which was theoretically possible. In time, there was such a normal, friendly working relationship throughout the entire commission that they were pleased when someone participated.

KRAUSS:

Cardinal König has a good name at the Vatican. Can you confirm, to the extent that you can say this officially, that he was a candidate for the papacy?

RAHNER:

I really don't believe that, because, as far as anyone knows who understands the matter, only at the last conclave was it even conceivable that a non-Italian might become pope. And that happened because the Italians couldn't agree on a candidate. Perhaps it was divine providence, but I do not believe that a non-Italian cardinal, much less a German-speaking one, had any chance of becoming pope until then. König certainly had the right stuff, especially his extraordinary fluency in languages, but I don't think he really had a chance. Some say that he was one of the pope-makers at the last conclave, but I'm not even sure of that. I never spoke to him about it.

KRAUSS:

John XXIII called you to be a theologian at the Council. What kind of a person was he? Indeed, they once thought him to be only a transition pope.

RAHNER:

Now, many papal legends have circulated about John XXIII praising him and playing him up. My fellow Jesuit, Burkhard Schneider, a church historian in Rome, who had access to the Vatican archives and had worked on Pius XII's political activity during the war years, told me that John XXIII is a typical example of how papal legends arise. He was basically an extraordinarily conservative pope, but humanly a very congenial one.

A Jewish designer in Rome once told me: "I spent half a year with Albert Schweitzer in Lambarene, but only now have I seen a saint," namely, John the XXIII. But for reasons that totally escape me, divine providence or historical circumstance, if you like, inspired this pope, in all his courageous innocence, with the idea of calling a new council. I believe that John XXIII had no idea what course this council should take, except for a few very general ideas. Just before this, he held a local synod in Rome and approved it in a reactionary and old-fashioned way. He allowed himself to be maneuvered into solemnly reaffirming Latin as the language of the Church, but the very opposite resulted, that is, nowhere is Latin used in the Church anymore except in official Roman documents. But John was an unusually likeable, honest person who could laugh at himself and who—I say this very simply—was used by God's providence to call the Council, a thing that Pius XII would never have dared and would probably have even considered superfluous.

KRAUSS:
Professor Rahner, did an era come to a close with the calling of the Council, and if so, how would you describe it?

RAHNER:
A quite definite era came to an end, an era I have called "pian."

KRAUSS:
After the popes called "Pius"?

RAHNER:
After the Pius popes, from Pius IX to Pius XII. A kind of defensive mentality, a certain defensive turning of the Church in on itself against the world, characterized this era in which the Church certainly had great missionary success, but in fact only by exporting Western European Christianity to all the world.

It was also an era of typical Latin neoscholasticism. Today, with the Second Vatican Council, the Church, I think, has expressly and consciously become a World Church. At the Second Vatican Council very many of the bishops from all over the world were really native bishops, enculturated in their own milieus. I also believe that one can say that neoscholastic theology and philosophy, for all their accomplishments, are quite passé today. During the Council or in the time of preparation for the Council, a theology different in its method and mentality was born. The Church decided to seek a more positive and a more active relationship with other Christian denominations. She discovered a more benevolent, more positive relationship with the other great religions of the world. In short, I believe there really is a new era in the Church.

KRAUSS:
In 1965 Pope Paul VI solemnly closed the Second Vatican Council. What kind of a person was he?

RAHNER:
Paul VI was an extremely urbane, cautious, personally unassuming man and Christian, who certainly suffered a great deal from his awesome responsibilities. He was initially, perhaps by nature, somewhat of a procrastinator, someone who hesitates. But in the circumstances, once urged by his sense of responsibility, he occasionally made decisions and took courses of action that even those with unconditional loyalty and the best of will toward the Roman papacy considered unfortunate. But I believe that we will gradually come to recognize that he was still an important pope.

Much that he did he had to do. He had to put up with many things simply because that was the way things were. But he did accomplish much by his trips, by his appearance at the United Nations, by his very active moves in ecumenism, especially in his relationship with the Orthodox Patriarchs—things that would have been almost impossible before him.

If you consider, for example, that he took the wholly un-thinkable step of deciding that cardinals lose their right to vote and have to retire when they reach the age of eighty. That is perhaps a small matter that doesn't excite others, but for Rome it was a colossal affair that rubbed many cardinals the wrong way, and they protested vehemently at the time. Now there are retired cardinals, so to speak. Furthermore, Paul VI allowed bishops to retire when they turned seventy-five and recommended that they petition Rome for this. Evidently, he once even considered resigning as pope and making room for a new papal election. In retrospect, all these are things that we perhaps take for granted. Previously, however, they were incredibly courageous steps.

KRAUSS:
What is the lasting significance of the Second Vatican Council?

RAHNER:
The Second Vatican Council is the first council of a World Church that really wants to be a World Church and not a Church with European exports to all parts of the world. And the Church of the Second Vatican Council has begun to become that World Church. This Council also brought to an end, or so I believe, a neoscholastic period of theology. This Council not only made a start in revaluating the role of the laity in the Church but also granted the bishops throughout the world, therefore the entire episcopacy, a greater role and importance in the Roman Catholic Church. Of course, one might still wish that this influence, that is, the importance and activity of

the entire episcopacy within Roman ecclesiology, were even greater yet.

In short, I do believe that the Second Vatican Council was a great council whose effects are not nearly at an end, a council that began a new era in the Church. One should not be so rash as to think or to suppose that ten years of conciliar measures should have already produced noticeable effects. It took the Council of Trent a hundred years to make itself felt in daily life. Of course, today things proceed much faster, because life today is faster. But the Second Vatican Council was a council that will never allow the Church to return to the way she was.

A CHURCH FOR
THE ENTIRE WORLD

KRAUSS:

Are you of the opinion, then, that European theology cannot be exported to other parts of the world, but that in Africa an independent, autonomous theology must come into being that can totally differentiate itself from our European theology?

RAHNER:

Yes, of course. Previously, with the evangelization that the Church is required to carry on throughout the world, European theology likewise had to be exported. Even today, most of the bishops in the world—in Africa, in Asia, and in Latin America—mainly studied in Rome. But if the Church really is or must become an actual World Church, not only in theory but in concrete life and practice as well, then clearly there will also have to be theologies in all the world that differ from a specifically European theology.

In time, an African, an Asian, and a South American theology must arise. These will be theologies of the one and the same faith. They will also understand themselves as always being under the Roman teaching office. But they will differ from the Western European theology that was, more or less, the only one in the Church, North America notwithstanding, until now. A certain pluralism in theology must exist simply because we are multidimensional human beings, and because the historical and cultural situations in individual countries are not the same. Nevertheless, theology must adapt to these culturally, historically, and even ethnologically different situations.

KRAUSS:

Does that mean that an independent theology could arise in Africa or South America that could reach totally different ethical decisions than we do in Europe?

RAHNER:

Well, of course this is a difficult question that I can't give a clear answer to off the top of my head. I would say that even in the ethical life there is a moral-theological pluralism of different life-styles that can be and is legitimate. Where the precise boundaries are for life-styles that can no longer be considered Christian, and where they are for a possible, concrete pluralism in ethical life-styles, is clearly a difficult question in individual cases.

To what extent can African marital ethics different from ours be legitimate for a Christian church in Africa? The human and the social situations are certainly different. Of course, this is a difficult question. Might it not be permissible for an African chief in the bush to have a harem, as did David and Solomon? Or is that absolutely impossible?

KRAUSS:

Would you allow the chief his harem?

RAHNER:

I don't know. I don't know enough about Africa. Of course, there is the additional difficulty that Asian culture, Indian culture, African culture are themselves undergoing extraordinary change. So, when I say that Africans can have marital ethics different in many respects from the Europeans', which Africans do I mean? Africans as they were a century ago, or Africans as they will exist in fifty years because of economic and other changes? There was the same problem in Turkey, independently of Christianity. If I am correctly informed, monogamous marriage is now a social value there too, although it was not in old Islam. Obviously, the Church doesn't need to revitalize old ethical life-styles that are now disappearing on their own.

KRAUSS:
With the Council, the Catholic Church opened its windows rather wide to the world. Doesn't there still exist now, some twenty years after the end of the Council, the danger that one window or another will be closed again? To put it another way, has stagnation entered the postconciliar period?

RAHNER:
You see, it can certainly happen that in a large house whose windows should be open there might be a closed window here or there. Otherwise there could be a bad draft. But I believe that there are indeed undesirable tendencies around, which is natural enough, of a restorative, conservative, or even perhaps reactionary sort, and that they can and should be overcome with time, but by and large the development that began with the Second Vatican Council cannot be reversed.

THE CHURCH
AND THE PAPACY

KRAUSS:

To what extent does the current pope play a part in this current stagnation? To what extent is he somewhat apprehensive about both the Church's opening up to the world and her opening up to other Christian churches?

RAHNER:

Well, first, I'm not really competent enough in this area to say. Second, I would say that it is self-evident that a pope's mentality and background would necessarily somehow enter into what he does as pope. I also have the impression that in this or that respect, the pope—I do not want to say that he is reactionary or conservative but that he has little sympathy perhaps for those things that a Western European values as irreversible progress.

But certainly we can say that the present pope is progressive in many ways. A South American theologian told me that the pope's talks on his South American trips were such that the liberation theologians, as they call themselves, could not have thought them out better themselves. That the pope doesn't especially like Communion in the hand, for example, is well known, but still he hasn't forbidden it and at least patiently tolerates developments like that.

KRAUSS:
You once said that you believed the current pope could still learn a thing or two. In which area does that seem desirable to you?

RAHNER:
Well, I can't go into that in detail now because I don't exactly know. But take this example: the present pope spoke about the Yahwist in a public talk, that is, about one of the many hypothetical authors of the Pentateuch. If he had spoken about the Yahwist like that as a biblical scholar in 1910, he would have been removed. Today even the pope himself regards such progress in Old Testament studies as self-evident. He no longer notices that he has a mentality that is totally different from the one officially allowed seventy years ago. Of course a pope can still learn something today. When he received the Dalai Lama yesterday, or whenever it was, these two gentlemen really talked to each other, and I can certainly imagine that the pope got an impression of Tibetan religion that he hadn't had before. And this can influence his decisions in a positive way.

So, let's allow each pope to have his own outlook. Let's not expect that each pope will have the call and the ability to make each and every thing in the Church better, especially when we aren't exactly certain, in this or that particular question, whether progressivism or conservatism is the better course. And if the pope does not fulfill all the promise that I or anyone else expects of him, is that really so bad? That's what happens in history and in a Church that changes only very gradually over the course of history.

KRAUSS:
Is the pope the highest representative of Christianity?

RAHNER:

I believe that you have to make a few distinctions. The pope is the highest representative of the Church and, if you like, of Catholic Christianity with respect to certain juridical, ecclesial structures. But I maintain that the most humble, the most loving (to put it in this old-fashioned way), the most holy, the most apparently obscure person in the Church, and not the pope, is at the top of the hierarchy, the real hierarchy for which the Church is only a means.

In his *Divine Comedy*, Dante, who is recognized by the Church as a great Christian poet, placed certain popes who did not please him in hell. That may have actually been unfair, but the highest representative within the social fabric is not necessarily the highest representative of the real reason for which the Church exists. She is there so that God may be worshipped, praised, and loved, and so that people might love one another and be selfless, and for that the saints are the real representatives. Innocent III was pope, but Francis of Assisi was the highest in the only hierarchy that ultimately counts.

KRAUSS:

In your opinion, when must the pope speak out and when would it be better for him to be silent?

RAHNER:

He should certainly be silent about matters in which he has no competence, and that a pope is not competent in everything is an obvious Roman Catholic truth, something always officially acknowledged and emphatically reaffirmed at the Second Vatican Council. In itself, this is a self-evident principle.

Of course, the question comes up in specific instances whether a pope has or has not surpassed the limits of his competence and mission, and this is certainly possible. In this matter there will always be different points of view. Must I be delighted by the fact that the pope received Arafat? Or should I say, well, he would have been better off to leave that matter alone? Catholic Christians can argue and differ about that. The Second Vatican Council expressly confirmed that differences of opinion are possible, even when people are appealing to the same ultimate Christian principles in the Catholic Church. So I may say that the pope travels around too much, and some other Catholic may say that the pope should travel more and go everywhere. With regard to the question of Jerusalem, he can have an opinion that differs from mine, and so on. All this is certainly obvious.

KRAUSS:
And when the pope takes a position on sexual morality?

RAHNER:
Then again I must make a distinction. Theoretically, the pope could eventually, in certain circumstances, take a final, defined position that would be binding for a Catholic theologian, although one could still fight about what this position means and so on. As long as the pope has not done that, one can then, under certain circumstances and with all due respect for authentic but not defined moral-theological statements from Rome, have another opinion concerning the concrete norms of sexual morality.

KRAUSS:
That was another genuine Rahnerian piece of information!

RAHNER:
No! Ah, dear God, that's the way things are! Truth is certainly a rather complicated matter. And there are obviously

teachings that I must respect, that do indeed have weight, without my being able to make an absolute claim to their truth. If you consult a doctor, he might say to you under certain circumstances: "In my medical opinion and according to the latest medical knowledge, you should have an operation." And you will probably have it without the doctor's being able to guarantee that that's the only thing to do, without his being able to guarantee that you will survive the operation, and without the guarantee that you might be even better off without it.

Similarly, meaningful principles that nevertheless do not signify ultimate truth can exist even in the Church, *do* exist even in the Church. Under Pius X the Church taught something officially about the origins of the Pentateuch that has since turned out to be incorrect or not totally correct, as promulgated in those days. It is exactly like that in medicine or in physics or in God knows what other science, where there are theories that once had a certain validity. It made complete sense for those without better knowledge to accept those theories, and, despite that, such theories were still open to later revision.

KRAUSS:
So, even papal statements may contain error?

RAHNER:
Why, of course. Just in the last one hundred and fifty years, the Church's teaching office affirmed various things that in the meantime have turned out to be wrong. Not official, papal or conciliar, ex cathedra definitions, to be sure. But the German Bishops' Conference admitted and explicitly stated in a written statement that the Church's teaching office has erred in the last one hundred and fifty years in authentic but non-defined teachings.

WHAT IS
HAPPINESS?

KRAUSS:
You speak occasionally of "happiness." Happiness is certainly not a theological concept. What do you understand by "happiness"?

RAHNER:
Naturally, happiness is also a matter of eternal life as a life of bliss. Hence, it is absolutely a theological word. That the happiness of someone enjoying middle-class comforts is not, without further ado, happiness in the theological sense is self-evident.

KRAUSS:
Is a happy life to be had here and now on earth?

RAHNER:
By all means people have the right to struggle and provide for a happy life, to some extent at least, that is, as far as they can and as far as they do not violate the rights of others.

KRAUSS:
Would you say that your life is happy?

RAHNER:

On the whole, certainly. Of course disappointments, sickness, and the ever-approaching nearness of death belong to contemporary human life, too. If you consider those as negative moments with regard to the question of happiness, then I must naturally admit that I too am not absolutely happy in every respect. I am certainly allowed to cry and to be sad. And I mustn't want to explain away or suppress this or that unhappiness in my life.

But if you ask, then I must say that without my deserving it, without my earning it, God has so ordained my poor little life (I don't know why) that I am remarkably so much better off than some poor devil in Vietnam or the children who died from American napalm and the like. At present I am much better off than the Poles. In German society I have no need to see myself as persecuted and discredited, as a priest in Poland must. A Polish priest told me that he was absolutely unable to get medical insurance in Poland. When he is ill, he must prove that he can pay before he is allowed into a hospital. Therefore, in a certain sense, I am better off—I can't do anything about it—than many, many people in this world. I don't know why God has ordained it so. I often fear that I am too well off. On the other hand, I also can't say that I'm bursting with happiness at present, either.

EARTHLY
AND ETERNAL LIFE

KRAUSS:
Professor Rahner, the clock in the background gives me the opportunity to ask: What does time mean to you?

RAHNER:
One of my early theological works focused on death, and it certainly discusses the question of time in relation to death. But for me, time is ultimately the possibility to decide definitively about oneself in freedom. Time is a sort of open space that makes something like historical freedom possible.

KRAUSS:
A short time ago I was reading something and these words struck me forcefully: "Life is fullness, not time." May I ask you: When you look back on your own life, do you think you've had a full one?

RAHNER:
Well, if I look back on my life, then I can indeed say that I succeeded in this or that, that I experienced and did this or that, had this or that encounter as well as love, fidelity, and so on. To that extent, my modest, meager, short life has indeed had a certain obvious fullness, it you want to call it that.

On the other hand, anyone who reflects upon his life clearly observes that everything he has experienced will seemingly be taken away from him, that everything recedes into an unavailable past and into a mere something that once was. And this person believes and hopes that this life of his will come to meet him again in the genuine, final, purified fullness of God. Now we are certainly not destined simply to become blessed and graced by God someday in a way that is totally different, totally unexpected; rather the harvest of our earthly life will be inserted into God's life, our eternal life. Time must ripen. Time must fulfill itself, biblically speaking, not only in the entirety of human history but also in individual lives. And what is seemingly only past and gone must return to us renewed again as our own special blessedness in God's life.

KRAUSS:
How do you find old age?

RAHNER:
Well, there are many people, especially today, who speak about old age with praiseworthy and somewhat heart-rending eulogies. A peaceful, ripe old age, an old age with wisdom, a beautiful old age perhaps in which one reminisces, does exist. But, quite soberly, the sort of old age that steadily draws near to death exists too—an old age in which one is exhausted. There is an age at which a person has the impression, in one way or another, of being pushed along the rails of death, an age at which one painfully sees life coming to an end. I believe that a Christian must also cope with this age too, soberly and without illusions, because he does have a "hope," as Paul would say, "against all hope."

KRAUSS:
How do you cope with the fact that growing old brings with it a diminishment of energy?

RAHNER:
I can cope with this only if I patiently accept it. If I realize that I can no longer climb 15,000-foot mountains, then I'll simply stay at the base. And if I realize that I can no longer really do productive intellectual work six hours a day, then I'll simply work only two or three hours and be satisfied with that.

KRAUSS:
Could you also resign yourself to not being able to work for even half an hour a day?

RAHNER:
They say of Saint Albert the Great that at the end of his life he forgot all his magnificent theology, which even today is still being collected and published in new multivolume editions. He could only pray the "Hail Mary." Good, if this happens to you, then you must cope with it too. Once you are on your deathbed, then everything does indeed cease—perhaps even your ability to react to such a situation. If even this is taken from you, all the better. Then, I believe, you find yourself all the more in God's hands, and no longer in your own. And you are better protected and more secure in God's hands than where you think you must be in control at all costs.

KRAUSS:
Is loneliness also a part of growing old?

RAHNER:

To a certain degree, yes. One should not pity oneself in a lyrical way but soberly recognize that one lives in an environment that is livelier than oneself, that it has tasks at which one cannot work anymore. Unavoidably, therefore, one does become isolated to some extent. One must reckon with that. But if there were once desert fathers who in their youth deliberately withdrew to the desert in solitude and still found a meaning to life there in a praying relationship with God, then one can indeed cope with the loneliness of old age.

KRAUSS:

So, it is a matter not only of living life but also of affirming death?

RAHNER:

Ultimately, of course, one cannot anticipate death, not even by committing suicide, but to a certain extent, one can do something like anticipate death by practicing renunciation, by enduring loneliness, silence, and perhaps by forgetting oneself.

KRAUSS:

You used the word "suicide." I want to ask you: Shouldn't the Church be more compassionate and generous than she used to be toward the many who, for whatever reasons, die at their own hands? No one, not even a Christian, receives a guarantee with his mother's milk that he will be able to endure life.

RAHNER:

If he really cannot endure it anymore, that means, if he is no longer capable of making a really free decision about himself because of psychological and physiological circumstances and, in these circumstances, takes his own life, then he falls into the hands of the merciful God. In each generation of my own immediate family I have experienced this apparently arbitrary ending of one's life. Once I gave a close relative a church burial, and I certainly find that to be, ecclesially and religiously speaking, the obvious thing to do.

KRAUSS:
Unfortunately, that is not really obvious to many.

RAHNER:
Well, I suppose that one has to say to each Christian and to oneself: "You do not have the right to take your own life." And consequently one has to say to oneself: "You have to endure your life until the end determined by God for better or for worse. You must cope with your psychological difficulties." But when the opposite occurs, that's a totally different situation to judge than when I am capable of acting responsibly and facing the question of how to cope with my life.

KRAUSS:
Professor Rahner, are you afraid of death?

RAHNER:
I ought to have the right to be afraid of death. After all, Jesus also experienced this in the Garden of Olives. Right now, I have no dreadful fear of death. Thanks be to God I am still very well, right? But as I said, a final free surrender or a final stoic appeal, as if the fear of death were forbidden to a Christian a priori—that I cannot admit. I'll wait and see! If I am

afraid of death, then I shall hand myself over to God's grace; and if I am not afraid, then that is also good, right? Certainly there are people who die quite without fear. But then, if a death of one sort or another is ordained for a person, that too is just one more matter that falls outside of my competence.

THE FUTURE OF
THE WORLD, THE CHURCH,
AND HUMANITY

KRAUSS:
Professor Rahner, what must the Church of tomorrow look like so that she can continue to address humanity even in the future with her good news, with her mission?

RAHNER:
First off I would say that if I am really a believing Christian, then ultimately I cannot allow my Christian convictions to depend upon the approval of society and public opinion. I am convinced that God is triune. Now, I cannot take a poll to determine what percentage of the German people holds the same conviction, and then adjust my beliefs accordingly.

This is particularly true of all prognoses for the future and of all assessments made of the Church's opportunities for the future. If in forty years only ten percent of families have their children baptized, I would still say that for a child of Christian parents baptism is an indispensable and meaningful thing. But if you ask me further how I would imagine the Church of the future, then I would say: I want, wish for, and expect a Church —can I say it?—of exceptionally strong spirituality, of much livelier piety, a Church of prayer, a Church that praises God and does not think that God is there for us, but is convinced rather, in theory and in practice, that we are here to adore

107

God, that we have to love him for his own sake and not only for our's.

KRAUSS:

But hasn't this been the Church's mistake somewhat, that she always gave people the impression that they were principally there for God? That they had to obey the commandments—and then God would be gracious. Shouldn't the other side be emphasized much more, namely, that God is there for us, unconditionally there for us? Mightn't it be on this point that the Church's preaching fell short?

RAHNER:

Well, it is certainly true that God is our salvation, that God loves us, and that God extends his arms to us in a special way to take us up into his eternal life. But just as you can only really become happy with another person if you love this person for his or her sake alone and not for your own happiness, so there is a similar relationship between the human person and God. We must love God for His own sake—love—because He is the eternal, holy, blessed, incomprehensible God. And if we have this relationship with Him only then is He also the God of our happiness, the God of a loving, forgiving providence. The strange thing is that one can find something only when one does not seek it directly and for one's own sake. I'd like to say that this is a basic structure of human existence. In fact, this structure is actually implied by your question; it is at the bottom of it.

KRAUSS:

Professor Rahner, you once said that it can be more important to bring one of tomorrow's persons closer to the Church's good news than to preserve two of yesterday's in the faith. What does that mean concretely?

RAHNER:
That means for the Church that a good offense is the best defense. That old fact of experience is just as true for the Church as it is for other things. If the Church is only anxious about taking care of the small flock that she has today or tomorrow, if she does not have the courage to preach the good news of Jesus Christ and his Gospel to those who have not yet accepted it, then she will shrivel up in time. She will also lose those whom she has today.

In other words, it seems to me that a very good pastoral-theological axiom for every bishop and pastor would be: Don't worry about the people who still participate in Catholic life. If nothing else, go out and convert the people who have good will but also have the impression that the Christianity they've been offered does not make them happy. Convert them; convince the contemporary scientist and the like that Christianity not only exists and will exist but that it is even the good news for the future as such. That is, I believe, more important than a defensive, conservative Christianity that seeks only to preserve yesterday's ever-present remnant.

KRAUSS:
I want to pick up on the word "future." From time immemorial the notion of the future has belonged to the great themes of theology, and it is very suggestive that the contemporary person, even the secularized person, is more and more asking about the future, especially since the glittering dreams of progress have proven completely false. Professor Rahner, how do you see the future of our world, the Church, and your own life?

RAHNER:

Let me begin with my own future: It boils down more or less to the hope of a "noble peace," as a Protestant hymn says, for yet a few more years. It is a hope that can deceive. But then, even beyond all these earthly possibilities, hopes, and the like that I possess with a certain trembling and uneasiness, I have the hope of the absolute Future, God Himself. I would say that beyond all possible material, biological, or even humanly attainable spiritual evolution, I have the hope of eternal life.

I have this hope, even if I cannot actually imagine what eternal life will really be like. I know through the good news of the Christian message and I know from Jesus Christ that the absolute, everlasting, holy, eternally good God has promised Himself to me as my future. And because of that, I have a good hope, an unconditional hope that is still subject to temptation as long as I am here on earth and have negative experiences with life, with society, with people, and so on. That is self-evident. But till death's door I'll hold doggedly fast, if I may say so, to the belief that there is an eternal light that will illumine me.

And I hold the same for the earthly future of one's own people or of the world as a whole. I'm all for the courageous struggle for a better economy, for a better social future, and I believe that the person who is really convinced of this must take responsibility for this social obligation before the judgment seat of God. When all is said and done, believers cannot and must not allow people who do not believe in this absolute future to get the better of them.

I would say that if the world is destroyed by atomic weapons or slips further and further into economic misery, that would be all too horrible and frightful. And everyone is obliged before God's eternal judgment to do everything in his or her power to prevent such things from occurring. One day we must give a reckoning for this. But if a people or even humanity were to fall into the abyss, then I would still be firmly convinced—and I hope to keep this conviction—that even such an abyss always ultimately ends in the arms of an eternally good, eternally powerful God.